A Girl's Hairstyle H

# of Everyday Hairdos

Step-by-Step Instructions for 12

Simple, Stylish, and Beautiful Hairdos

By Abbi Robertson

ISBN-13: 978-1720820758

ISBN-10: 1720820759

All photos taken by Danielle Robertson

Acknowledgments

Thank you, my wonderful family, for helping me accomplish my dreams by letting me spend hours a day working on this book.

Thank you, Dad, for keeping my vision focused and thank you Mom for encouraging me to take care of myself and opening the door to the world of hair styling for me (although I may have gone through it kicking and screaming).

Thank you, my sister Dani, for using your photography skills to take the pictures in this book! They turned out way better than I imagined! Keep up the good work!

Thank you, my amazing "models", for being so patient with me and putting up with my amateur ways. You girls were awesome!

Thank you to my Creator who created me to be a beautiful light for His glory!

Contents

Why I Wrote this Book

Before I became interested in hairstyling, I was your average tween whose daily 'do rotated between a tight ponytail, a braid, or throwing on a headband. My mom would tell me to "go do something new" with my hair but I never could create anything and would just end up getting frustrated in front of the mirror. She encouraged me to keep trying and suggested I watch some hair tutorial videos. I watched them and would practice them on my sister and then practice doing them on myself. I became enthralled as I discovered styles that were easy, pretty, and I could do on myself. It wasn't long before I was coming up with my own way of wearing braids and updos.

When I would look for a new hairstyle to try, I would look for styles that were relatively easy, simple looking, and pretty; styles I would wear every day. I also looked for styles that were adaptable so that I could add in my own unique twist.

I have filled this book with just that - styles that are beautiful, easy, adaptable, and are definitely ones you can wear every day and not get tired of. The styles in this book are perfect for those who are beginning to take an interest in styling, whether you are a young girl trying to style your own hair, or a mom trying to do your daughter's hair (or maybe even your own).

For those who can relate with the frustration of learning how to style your hair, don't give up. I know it sounds cliché, but I am serious. All it's going to take for you to master these styles is some patient practice. Once you master them, get creative! Come up with your unique style using the styles from this book as your basis. That's why I wrote this hair styling book. I want to encourage you to take delight in looking your very best!

Let's begin!

What You Will Need:

Hairbrush: to smooth down hair and reduce flyaways (for flyaways see p.4).

Wide Tooth Comb: for detangling and straightening dry or wet hair.

Fine Tooth Comb: I use this comb to make parts and smooth down small sections of hair.

Hair-ties: also known as hair-bands; I prefer to use the cloth covered ones that are metal free. I use them to secure large portions of hair.

Hairspray: to assist in making sure the styles stay secure throughout the day.

Elastic Hair-ties: for securing small portions of hair or securing ends. I prefer to use clear elastics.

Bobby Pins: for pinning up loose strands of hair or holding pieces of hair in place. They come in three different sizes: large, medium, and small. Large works best for heavy, thick hair, and the small ones work great for securing hair without showing. There are also different color options to match your hair color.

Topsy Tail: A Topsy Tail is like a large needle which you can thread your hair through to create flips in a style. You can find a Topsy Tail at a beauty supply store or online.

Spray Bottle: fill with water to spritz on hair to tame flyaways.

Bun Former: a great tool to create the perfect bun. It works with all hair types. You can get one at a beauty supply store or online.

Curling Iron or Wand: I prefer to use a 1-1 ½ inch curling wand when curling hair for some of the styles in this book. FYI: What's the difference between a wand and an iron? An iron has a clamp piece while a wand has just the barrel.

Styling Terms and Tips

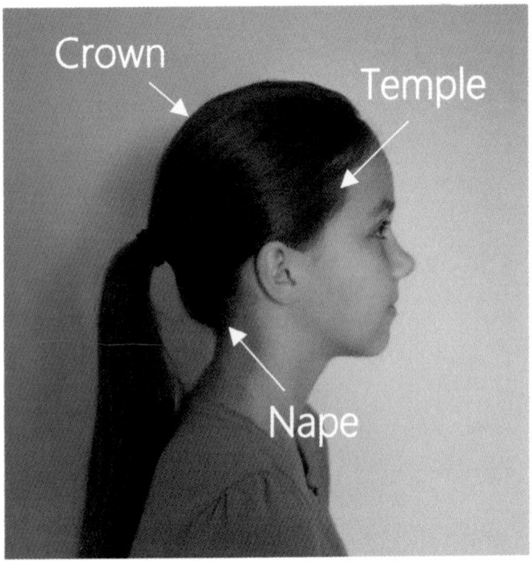

Flyaways: While it may be an unofficial term, flyaways are short, loose hairs that stick out of a style. If you are going for a more sleek, smooth look, flyaways can be a problem. An easy way to take care of flayaways is to spritz a fine-tooth comb with hairspray, and then comb the flyaways down.

Heavy Side of the Part: When you part your hair to the side, you will have one side that has more hair than the other. The side with the most hair is called the heavy side of the part.

Pancaking: Starting at the tail end of the braid, gently pull on the outside edges of the braid. This is pancaking. Continue pancaking up to the top of the braid. Pancaking makes the braid flatter, hence the term pancaking. It also gives a softer, fuller look to the braid.

Rotation: A completion of certain steps which you repeat over and over to finish a braid.

Basic Braids

To complete some of the styles in this book, you will need to know the basics. Be patient and practice, and before you know it you will be ready to create beautiful 'dos.

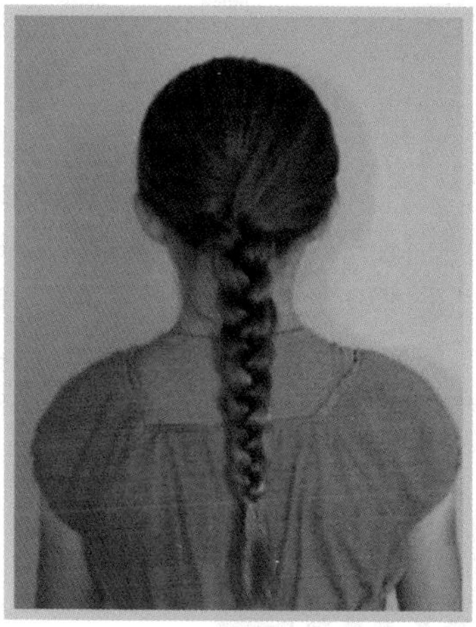

3-Strand Braid
p. 6

French Braid
p. 7

Dutch Braid
p. 10

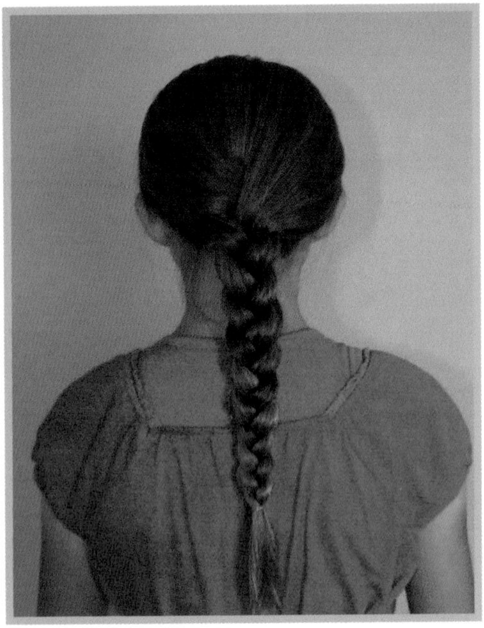

3- Strand Braid

This basic braid is one of the techniques that is essential to any braided style.

1. Divide hair into three equal strands.

2. Take the left-hand strand of hair and cross it OVER the middle strand, trading places.

3. Take the right-hand strand of hair and cross it OVER the new middle strand, trading places. You have completed one "rotation" of a 3-strand braid (for rotation see p. 4).

4. Repeat steps 2-3 until you run out of hair to braid. Tie off ends with an elastic hair-tie.

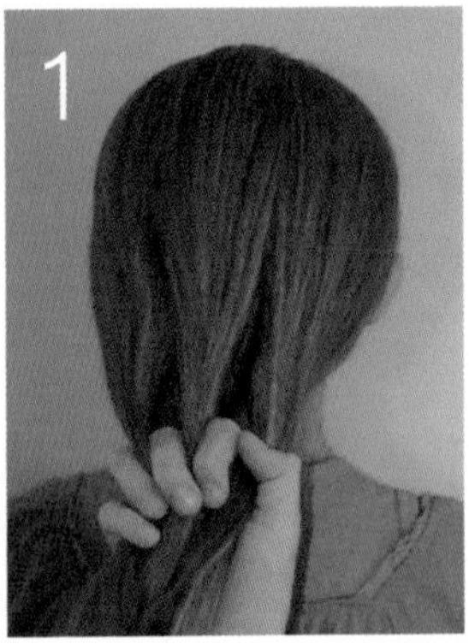

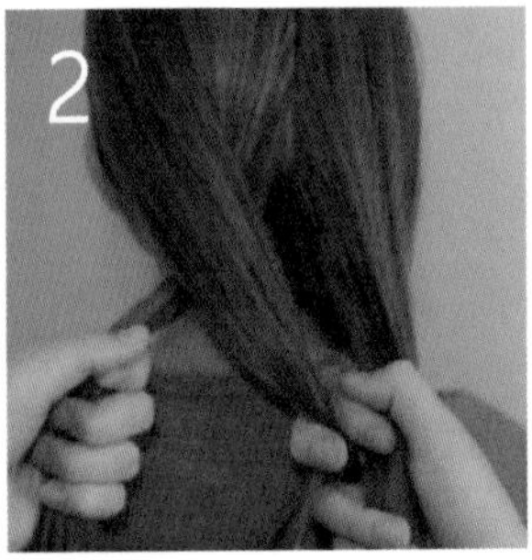

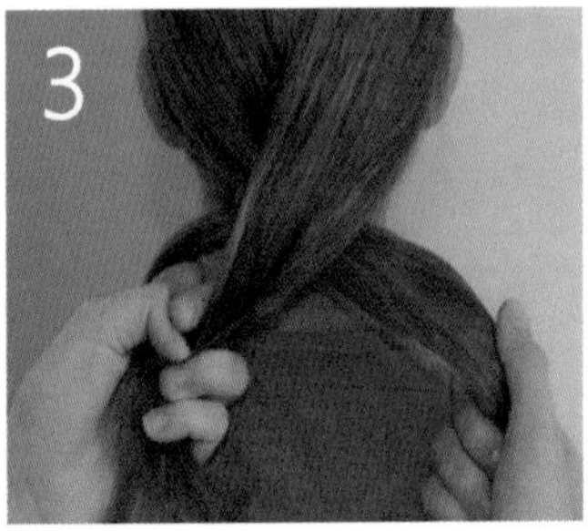

French Braid

While it may seem hard and complicated at first, the French Braid is a fairly simple braid that only requires some patient practice in order to master it. Think of it in a pattern: braid - add in hair to outer strand – braid – add in hair to outer strand - etc.

1. Start by grabbing the hair by the temples and gathering all the hair from that point up into a high half-up.

2. Divide the half-up into three equal strands.

3. Cross the left-hand strand of hair OVER the middle strand, trading places.

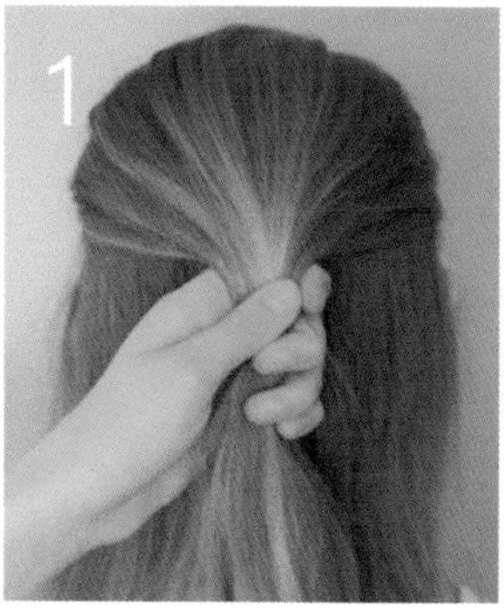

4. Then cross the right-hand strand of hair OVER the new middle strand, trading places.

5. Holding what you have already braided in one hand, use your other hand to grab a section of hair from the front left. Add this section to the hair in the left-hand strand.

6. Now cross the left-hand strand, the strand you have just added hair to, OVER the middle strand, trading places.

7. Now grab a section of hair from the front right and add this section of hair to the hair in the right-hand strand.

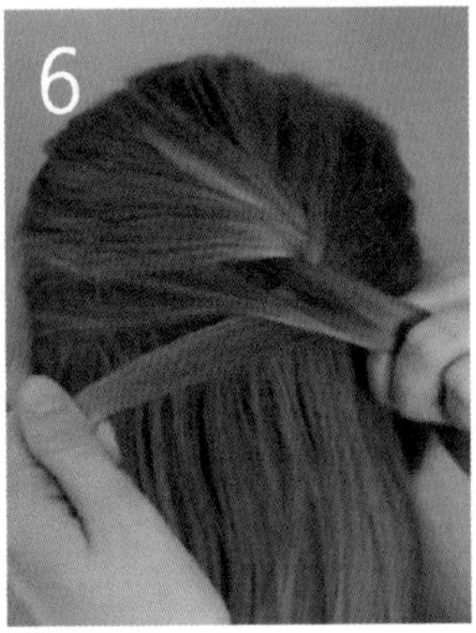

8. Cross the right-hand strand, the strand you have just added hair to, OVER the middle strand, trading places. You have completed one "rotation" of a French Braid.

9. Repeat steps 5-8 until you have brought all of the hair into the braid.

10. When you have incorporated all of the hair into the braid, braid the remaining hair in a 3-Strand braid. Secure ends with a clear elastic.

Hair Variation

Create two French braids by making a part going down the middle of the head to create two equal sections of hair. Starting with one of the sections, take a piece of hair from the front, near the part line, and divide it into three pieces. From there continue as with a normal French Braid. Repeat with other section.

Dutch Braid

Once you have mastered the French braid, the Dutch braid is very simple. It is basically a French braid, but in reverse.

1. Start by grabbing the hair at the temples and gathering all the hair from that point up into a high half-up.

2. Divide the half-up into three equal strands.

3. Cross the left-hand strand of hair UNDER the middle strand, trading places as shown in picture 3a. Then cross the right-hand strand of hair UNDER the new middle strand, trading places as shown in picture 3b.

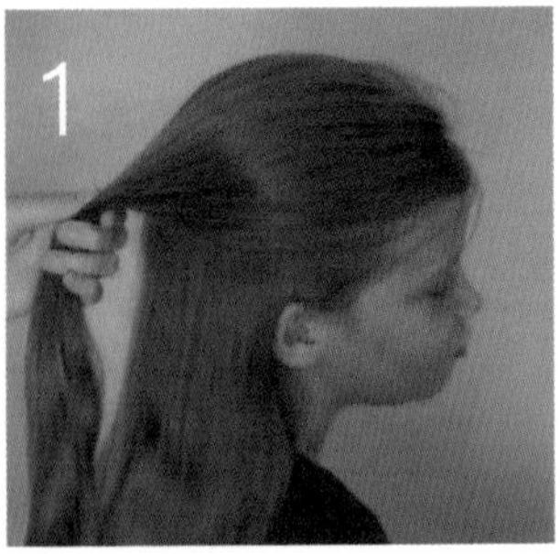

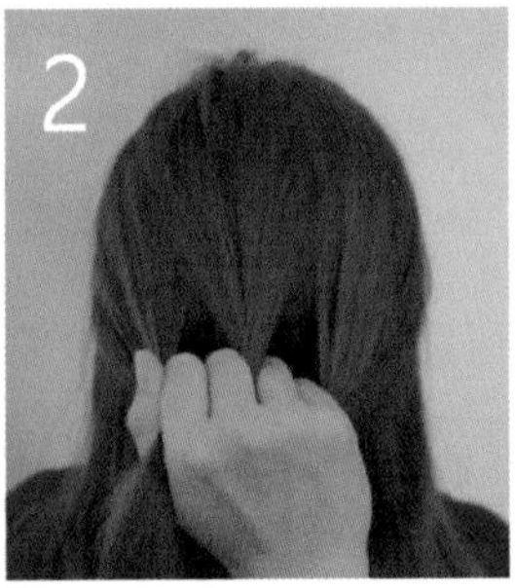

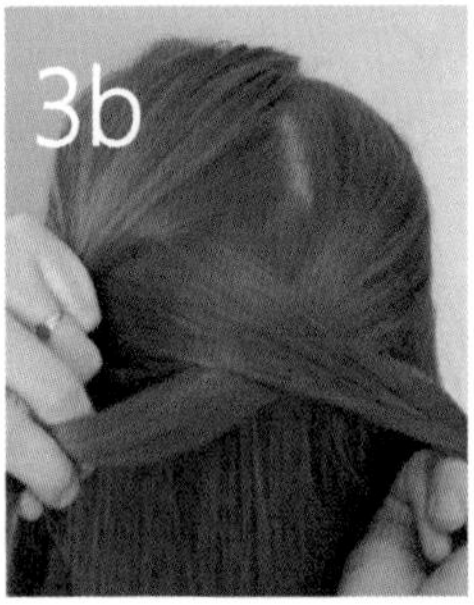

4. Holding what you have already braided in one hand, use your other hand to grab a section of hair from the front left. Add this section to the hair in the left-hand strand.

5. Cross the left-hand strand, the strand you just added hair to, UNDER the middle strand, trading places.

6. Now grab a section of hair from the front right and add this section to the hair in the right-hand strand.

7. Cross the right-hand strand UNDER the middle strand, trading places. You have completed one "rotation" of a Dutch Braid.

8. Repeat steps 4-7 until you have brought all of the hair into the braid.

9. When you have incorporated all of the hair into the braid, braid the remaining hair in a 3-Strand braid, but in reverse, which is crossing the outer strands UNDER the middle strand. Secure ends with a clear elastic.

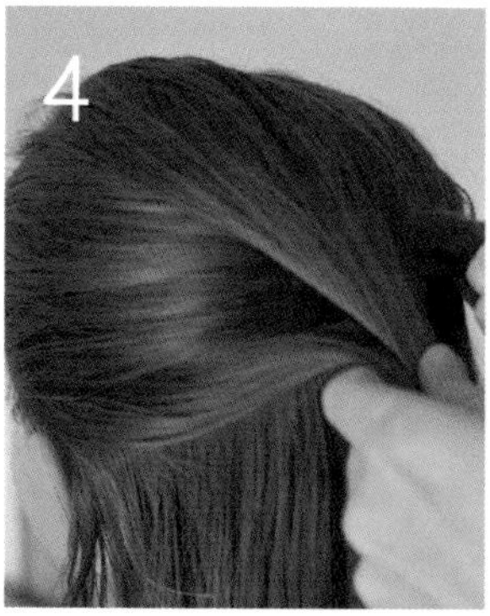

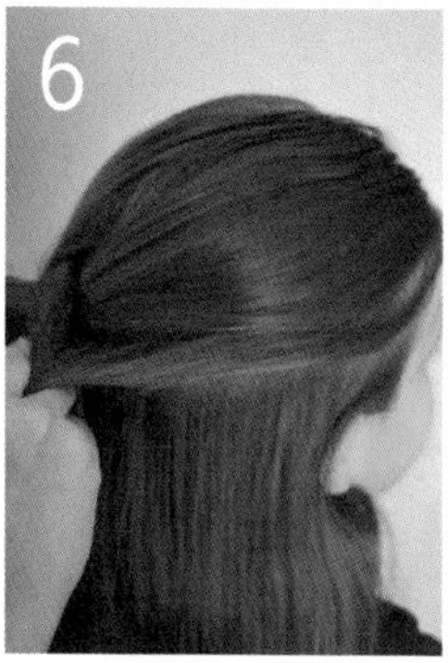

Hair Variations

Something I like to do is pancake the edges of this braid. It gives the braid a soft, loose look and also makes it seem fuller.

Everyday Styles

Now that you have practiced the basics, you are ready to create the styles.

These styles are simple, pretty, and are definitely ones that you can do, even on those days when you are on the run. For most of the styles I give suggestions on how to create variations of the style or how to achieve a certain look. There are so many possibilities that you never should tire of wearing these styles over and over again.

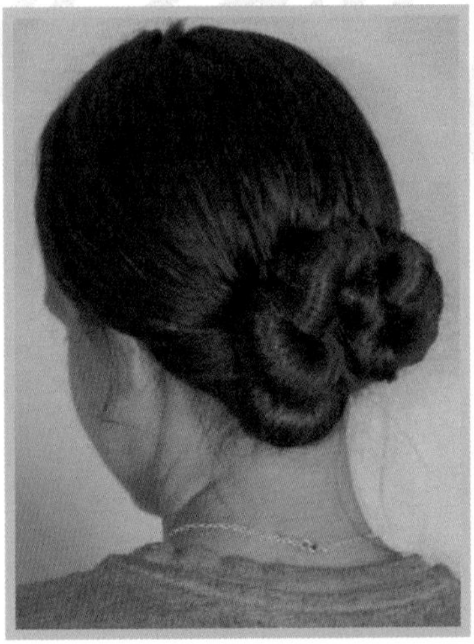

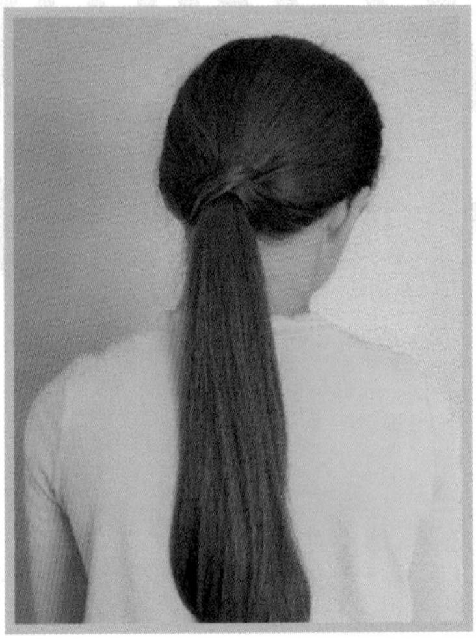

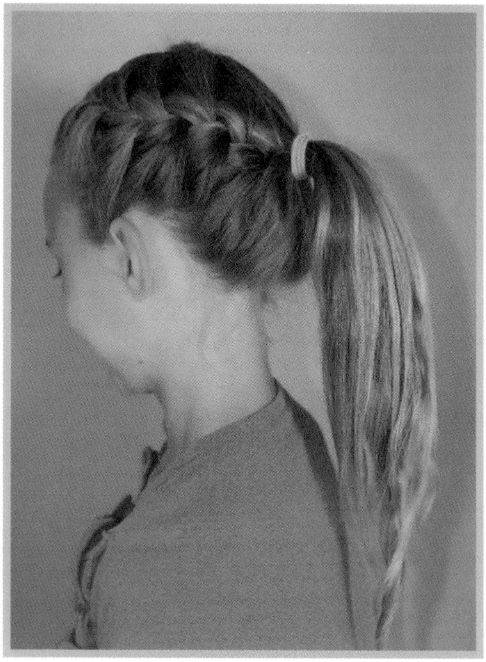

French Braid Pony

Tired of that plain pony that you always wear? Here is a style that adds some extra cuteness and gives your pony a little more of an edgy look.

1. Make a part on the right side of the head. Take a piece of hair from the front, left side of the part.

2. Divide the section of hair into three equal strands. Begin creating a normal French Braid (p. 7-10) as shown in picture two.

3. While French braiding, braid the hair so that it swoops down more towards the ear (see picture).

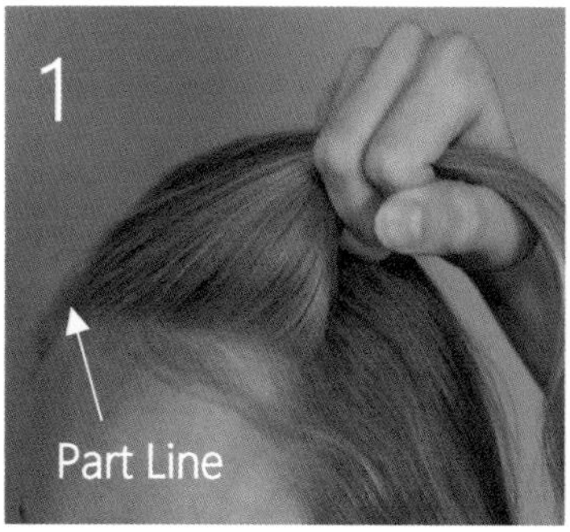

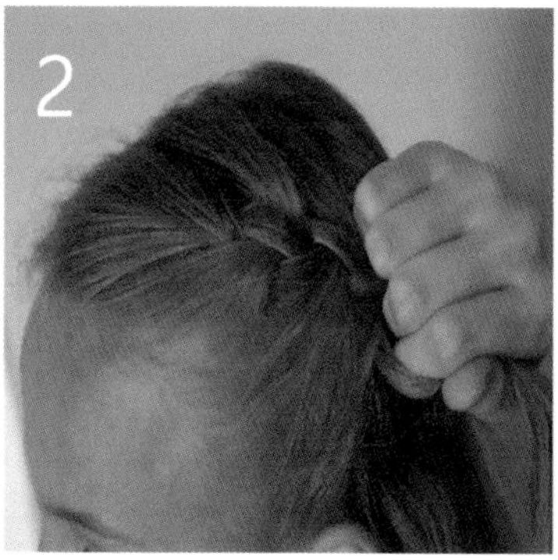

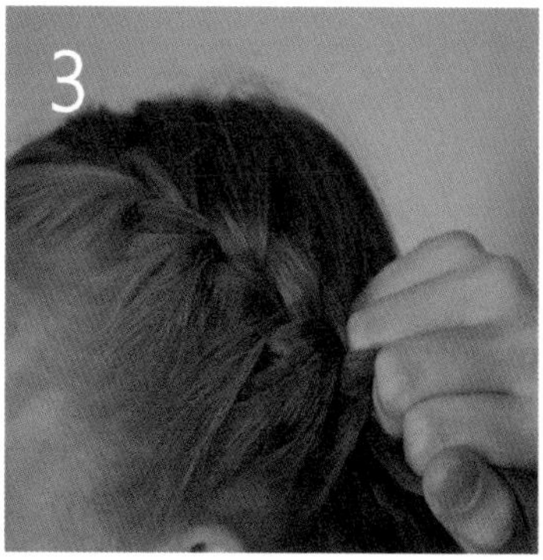

4. Continue braiding in a slightly curved pattern, until you reach the middle of the back of the head, or until you reach where you will place your pony-tail.

5. Stop adding in sections of hair and continue braiding in a 3-strand braid. Secure the ends of the braid with a hair-tie.

6. Gather all of the remaining hair and pull it into a smooth pony-tail. Add the braid to the pony, placing it on top of the pony-tail. With a hair-tie, secure the pony-tail and braid.

7. Undo the hair-tie at the end of the braid and unbraid until you get to the top of the pony-tail.

Hair Variation

The awesome thing about this braided 'do is that it is so adaptable. Instead of leaving it in a pony, you can wrap it into a bun. Or try doing a double braided pony repeating the steps on the right side of the head and combining both braids into a pony. You could even try this style using a Dutch braid.

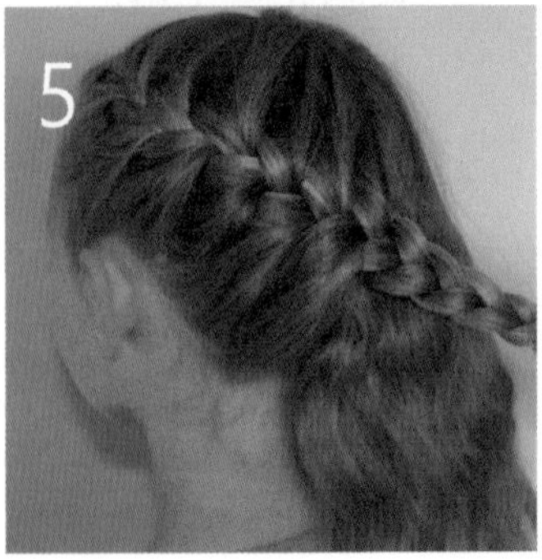

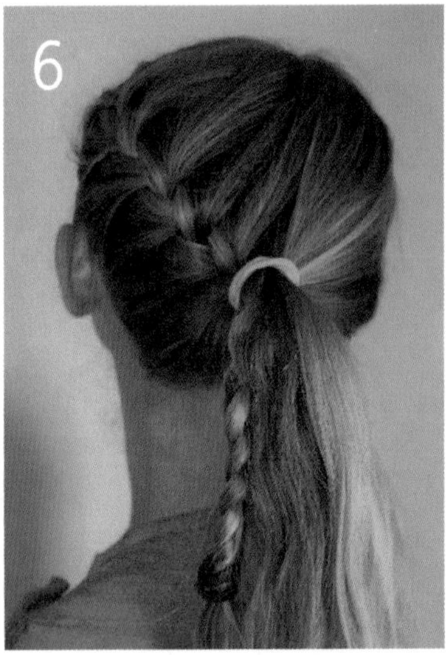

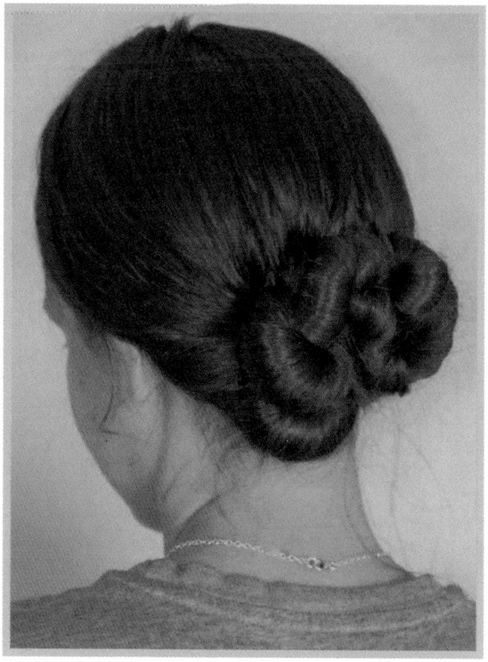

Twisty Bun

This style is not only cute, but simple. There is no way to go wrong with this bun and it only takes three minutes to create.

1. Spray hair with water so that the hair is damp. Gather all of the ends of the hair and tie them together with a clear elastic, leaving about a 2 ½ inch tail (see picture).

2. Divide all the hair above the elastic into two equal sections. You can use a comb to help make it more even.

3. Flip the ends up and through the space between the two sections of hair.

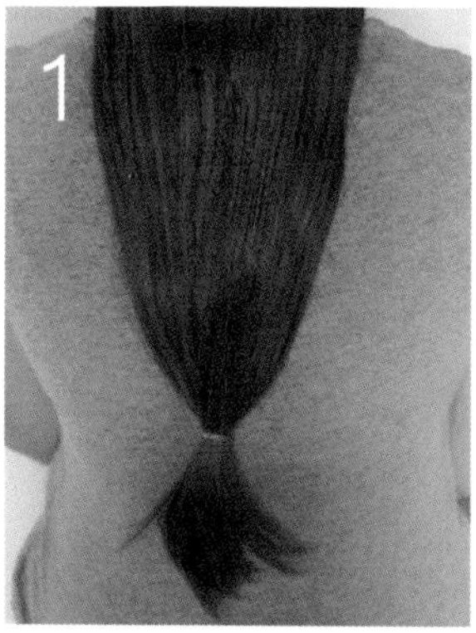

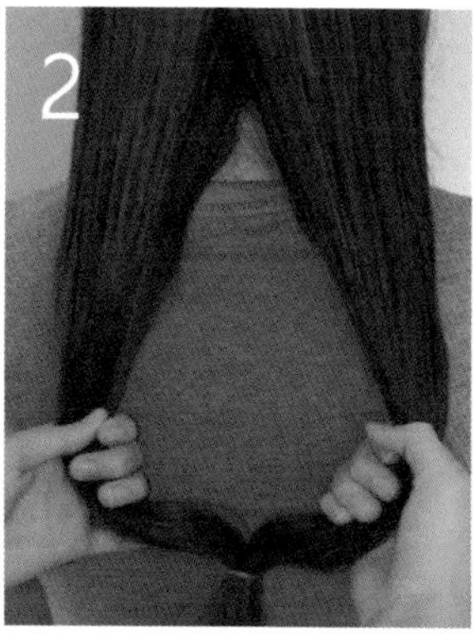

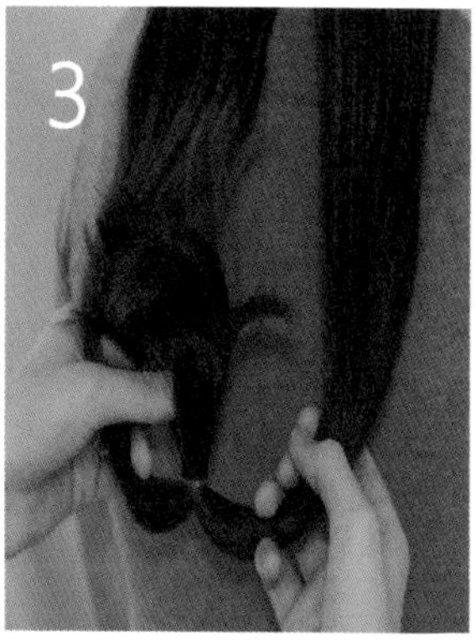

4. Repeat step 3 until the twists are kinked up at the nape of the neck.

5. Pull the ends up so that the twists are below (see picture.)

6. Twist the ends and tuck them underneath the Twisty Bun. Bobby pin the twisted ends securely.

7. Now pin the Twisty Bun so that it lies flat against the head.

Hair Variation

This style can also become an alternative to the Messy Bun (p. 32). Just pull and loosen the twists after pinning up the bun.

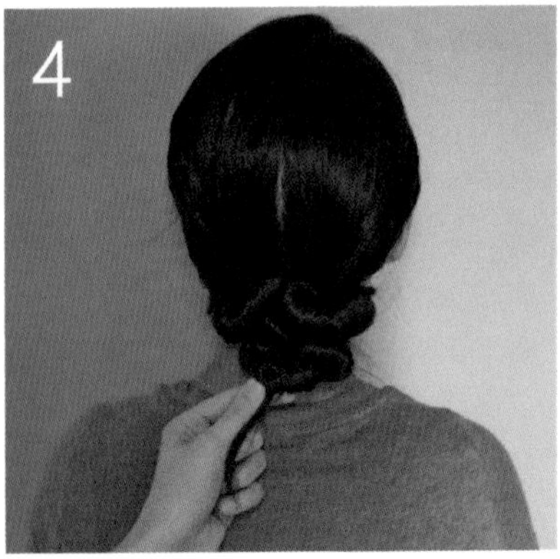

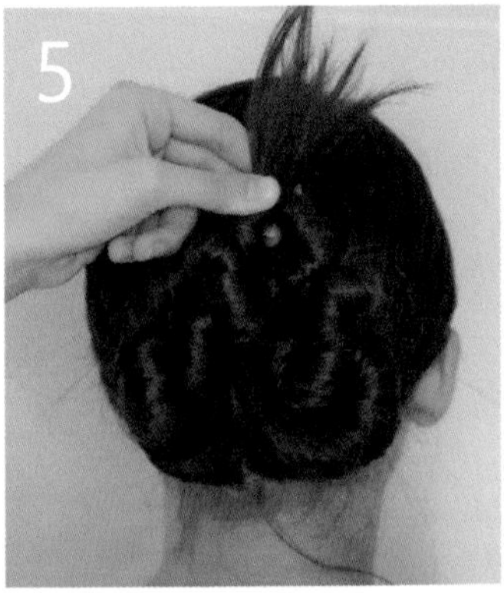

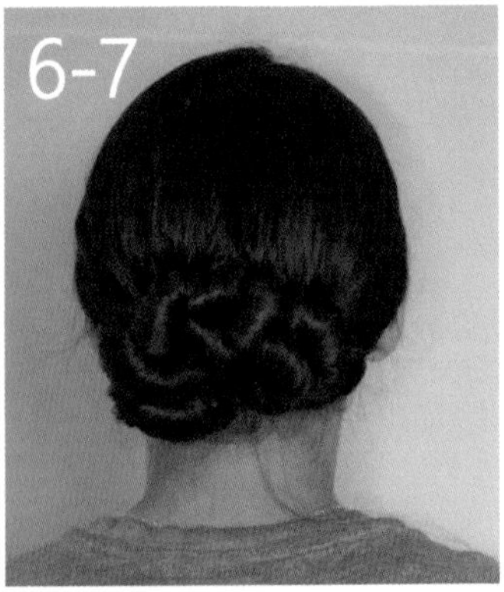

Diagonal Dutch Braid

While it may look difficult, this braid is just taking what you already know and taking it to the next level.

1. Make a part on the right side of the head. Take a piece of hair from the front left side of the part.

2. Divide the section of hair into three equal strands.

3. Begin creating a Dutch braid (p.10-11). For the first two rotations, keep the braid following the front hairline (see picture).

4. After you have done your first two rotations, stop following the hairline and continue braiding at a slight angle downward (see picture).

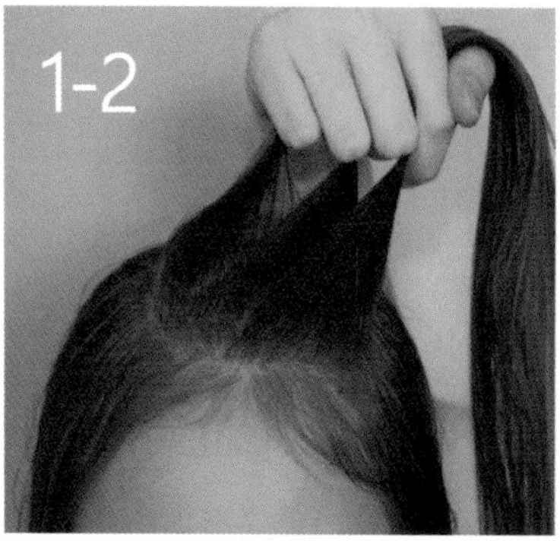

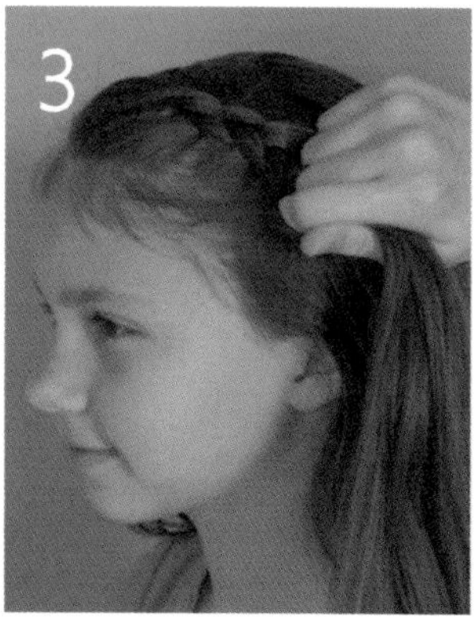

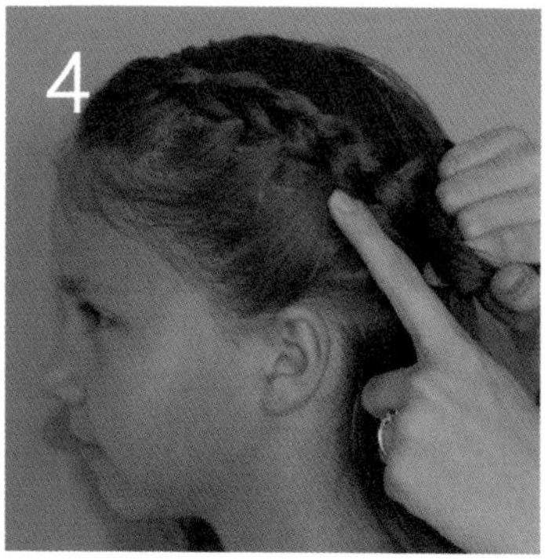

5. Continue braiding across the back of the head. Keep braiding down at a slant so that you get that diagonal look. The back of the head is where the angle is really going to show.

6. By the time you have brought all of the hair into the Dutch braid, you should end up at the nape of the neck just behind your ear. Braid all the remaining hair into a 3-strand braid remembering to continue crossing the outer strands UNDER the middle strand.

7. Secure ends with an elastic hair-tie. If desired, go back and pancake the edges of the braid.

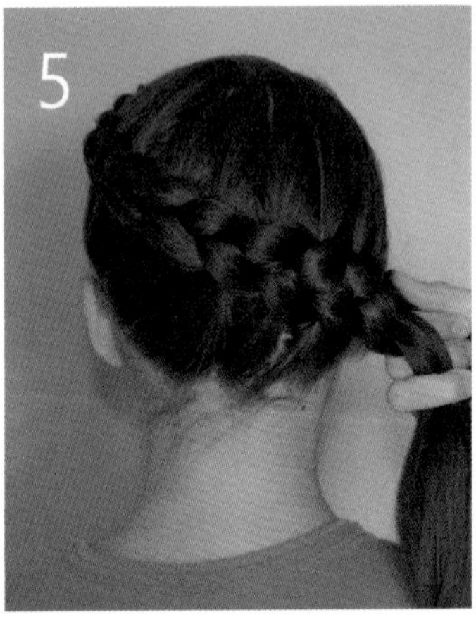

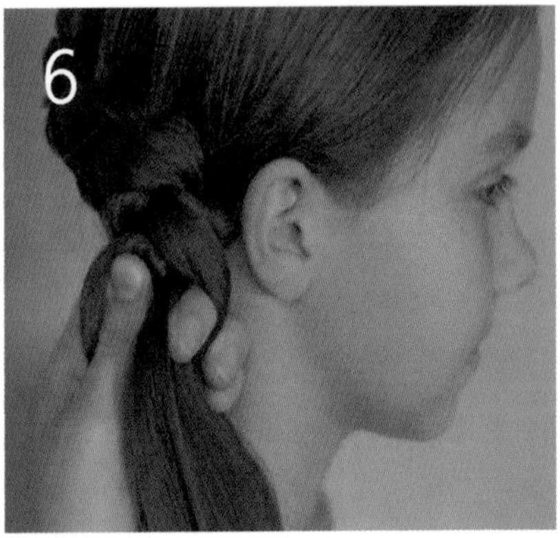

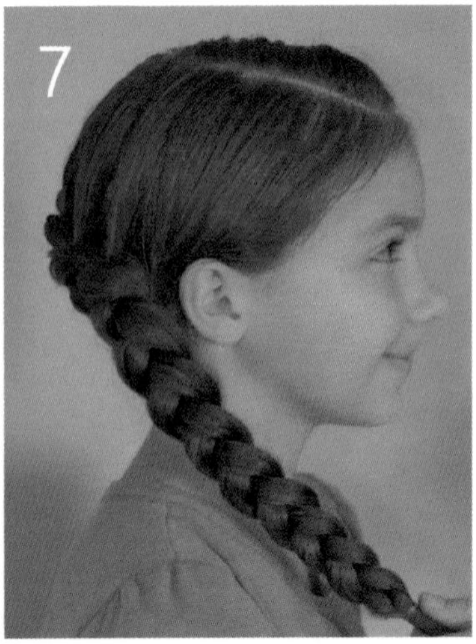

Alternative Braid

This amazing braid is not a braid at all! It is actually made out of twists.

1. Sweep all of the hair to the side. Divide the hair into two equal sections.

2. Twist the two sections of hair towards the middle, or towards each other.

3. Once you have a couple inches of twisted hair, bring the two twists close beside each other.

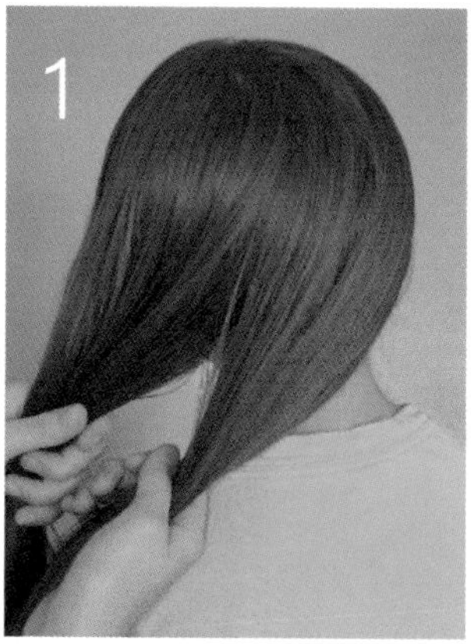

4. Using your index finger, push through the side of one of the twists, going all the way through the other twist. You now have a section of hair above and below your index finger. Hold the top section between your thumb and index finger. Release the hair in your other hand (see picture 4a). Grab the bottom section and separate it from the top (see picture 4b).

5. Twist the two sections towards each other again as before.

6. Continue steps 4-5 until you can no longer make twists.

7. Secure ends with an elastic hair-tie.

Hair Variations

Want to go for a Bohemian messy look? Pancake the edges of the braid and leave some loose hairs around your face for a sweet look.

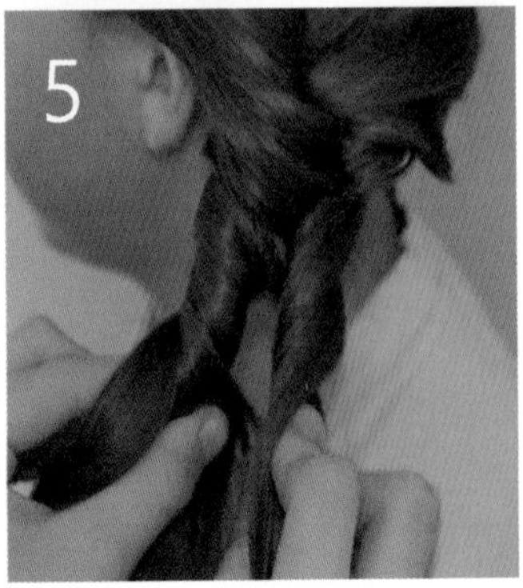

Dutch Half-Up

Whether you have long or short hair, this is your next "go to" style. It is suitable for any occasion, fancy or casual.

1. Make a part on the right side of the head. Take a section of hair from the front, on the left side of the part.

2. Divide the piece of hair you have just sectioned off into three equal parts.

3. Begin creating a Dutch braid (p.10-11). For the first two rotations, keep the braid closely following the front hairline (see picture).

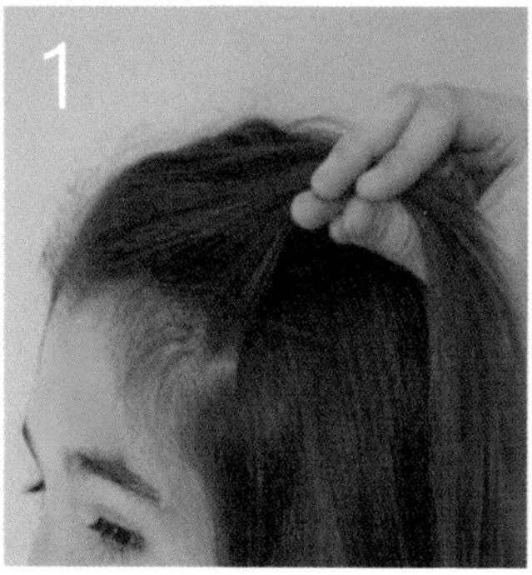

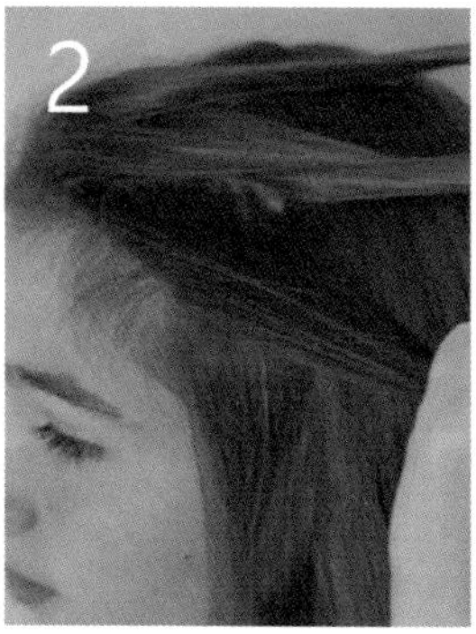

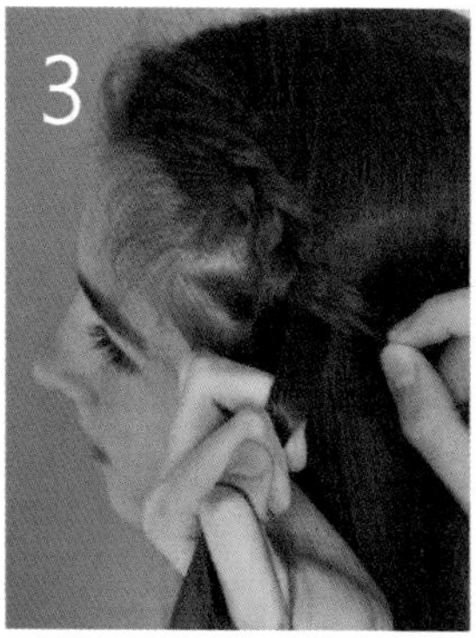

4. After you have done your first two rotations, continue braiding in a slight downward curve (see picture).

5. Once you have braided past the ear, stop Dutch braiding and begin braiding a 3-strand braid remembering to continue taking the outer strands UNDER the middle strand.

6. Stop braiding when you reach the middle of the back of the head. Secure the ends of the braid with a hair-tie.

7. Repeat steps 1-6 on the right side of the head.

8. Now that you have two Dutch braids, one on either side of the head, secure them together with a clear elastic. Pancake the edges of the braid to create a fuller look.

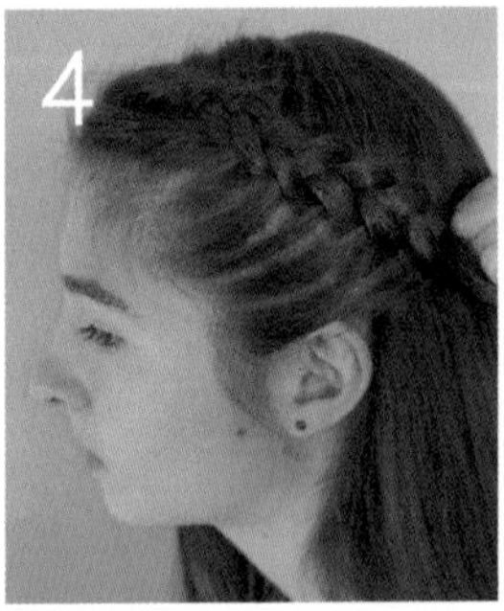

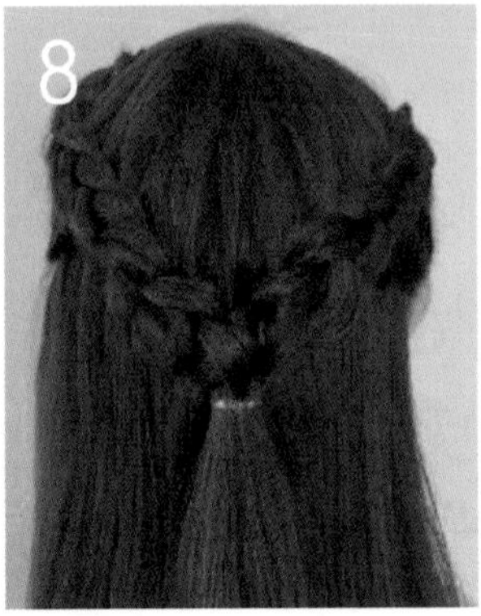

9. Take a small piece of hair from the pony and wrap it around the elastic hair-tie so that it hides it. Wrap hair around elastic until you have 2-4 inches left.

10. Using your finger or a Topsy Tail, tuck the end of the piece of hair into the top of the half-up, and bobby pin in place. If you use a Topsy Tail, insert pointed part into the hair above the elastic hair-tie. Thread the piece of hair through the loop at the top of the Topsy Tail and pull down through the hair.

11. Optional Step

Curl the rest of the hair with a curling wand or iron, on a low to medium heat setting.

Hair Variation

For a Boho look, leave two French braids in overnight so that they give your hair a wave. Take out the French braids and complete the Dutch Half-Up. Pancake the edges of the braids.

Waterfall Twist

Here is another easy, three-minute style for you! You'll love how easy and effortless it is to create.

1. Create a part on your preferred side. Take a piece of hair from the top front on the heavy side of the part (the side with the most hair) and lightly spray it with water. Divide this section into two equal parts.

2. Cross the bottom strand up and over the top strand.

3. Now take a small piece of hair from above the twist and place it over the top strand and through the middle of the two strands of hair (see picture).

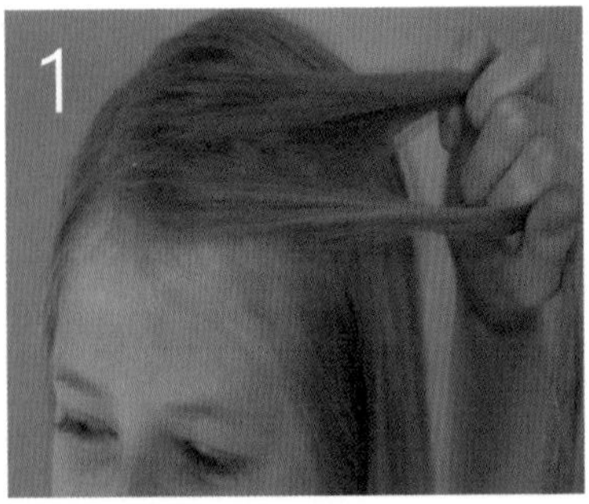

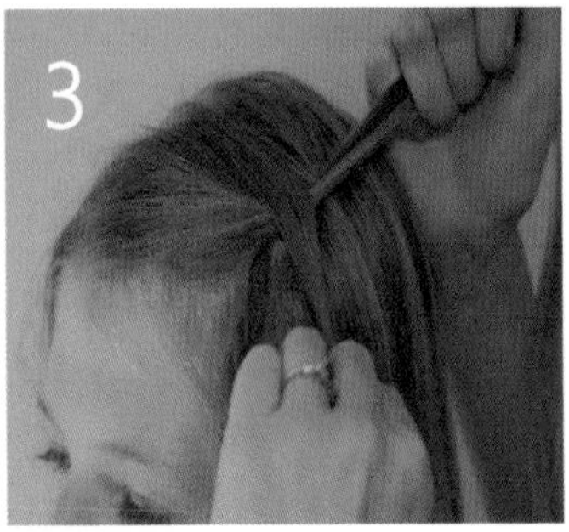

4. Cross the bottom strand up and over the top strand, locking the piece of hair that is in between securely. Let the piece of hair added in between the two strands drop.

5. Repeat steps 3-4 until you reach the desired length.

6. To complete the Waterfall Twist, after you place the last piece of hair through the middle of the two strands, cross the bottom strand up and over the top strand and repeat again to ensure that the twists stay tight.

7. Secure the Waterfall Twist with a clear elastic.

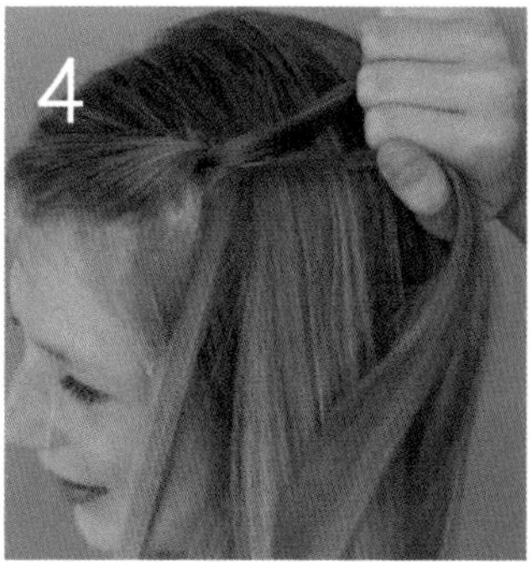

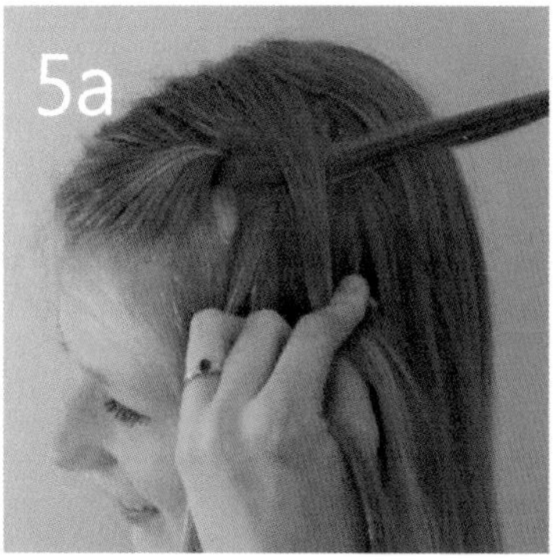

Hair Variation

Try creating a Double Waterfall Twist! Take a section of hair from the temple just below where you started the first Waterfall Twist. Make sure not to include the strands of hair "falling" through the first Waterfall Twist in that section. Begin a normal Waterfall twist. When you go to place a piece of hair between the two strands, take the strand of hair falling from the first twist and place that in between. When your second Waterfall Twist is the same length as the first one, combine the two ends, and then secure them with a clear elastic.

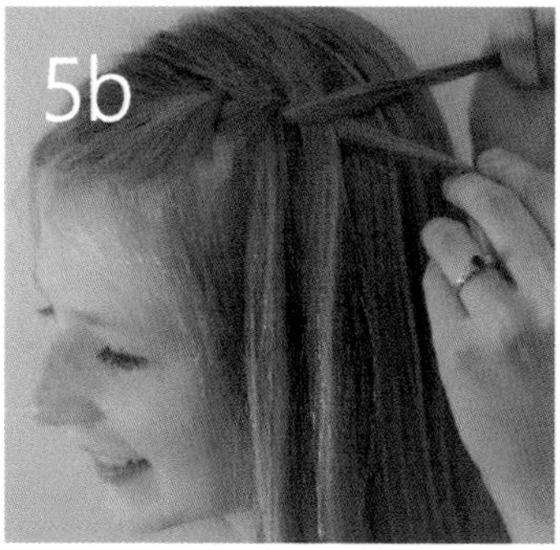

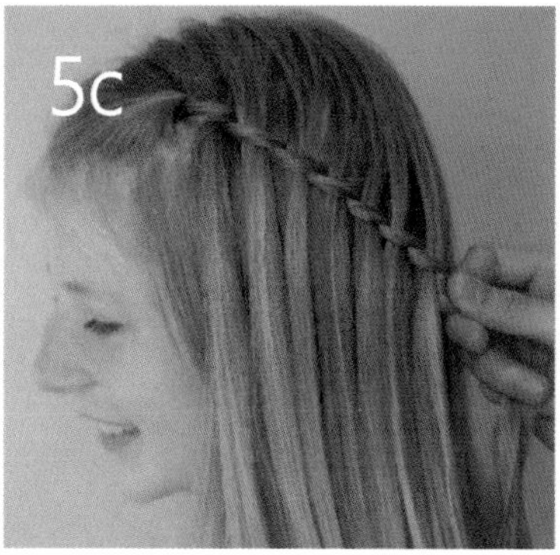

Twist and Side Braid

A new and cute way to add an extra "twist" to a simple 3-strand braid.

1. Create a part on your preferred side. The braid will be on the heavy side of the part.

2. On the heavy side of the part, section off a piece of hair from the front near the part line (see picture 2a). Divide this piece into two equal strands (see picture 2b).

3. Twist the two strands together by taking the bottom strand and crossing it up and over the top strand.

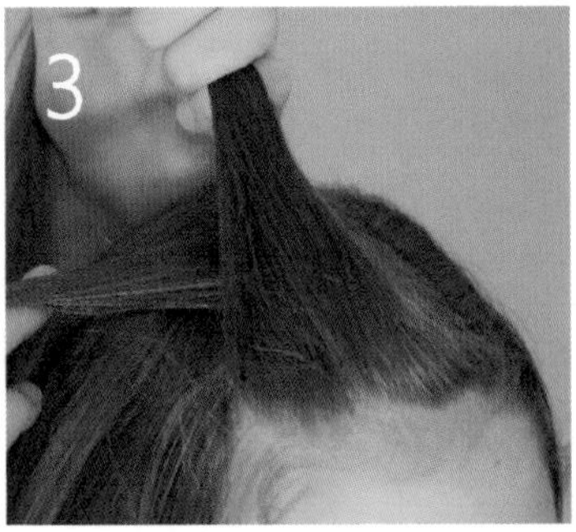

4. Take a piece of hair from underneath the twist and add it to the bottom strand. Now cross the bottom strand up and over the top strand.

5. Continue the pattern from step 4, twisting at a slight downward angle, and stop just behind the ear.

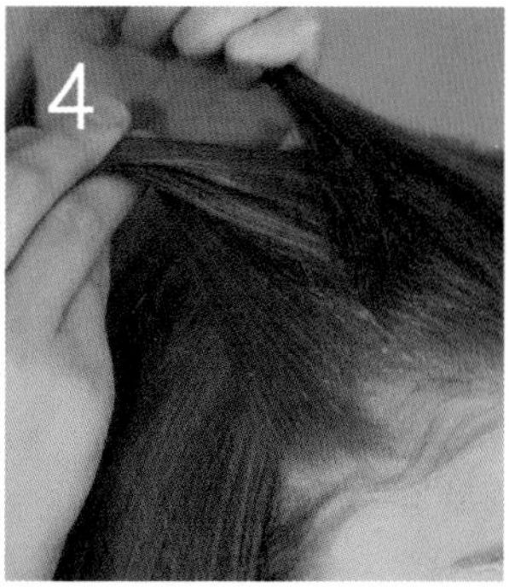

6. Sweep all of the remaining hair to the side where the twist is.

7. Combine all the remaining hair and the hair in the twist together and divide the hair into three even sections for a 3-strand braid. Braid until you run out of hair. Tie off the end of the braid with a clear elastic.

Hair Variations

Instead of a 3-strand braid, try a Fishtail Braid (p. 34).

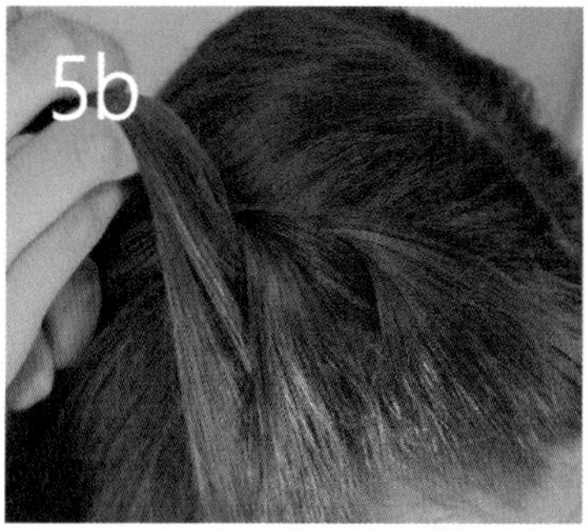

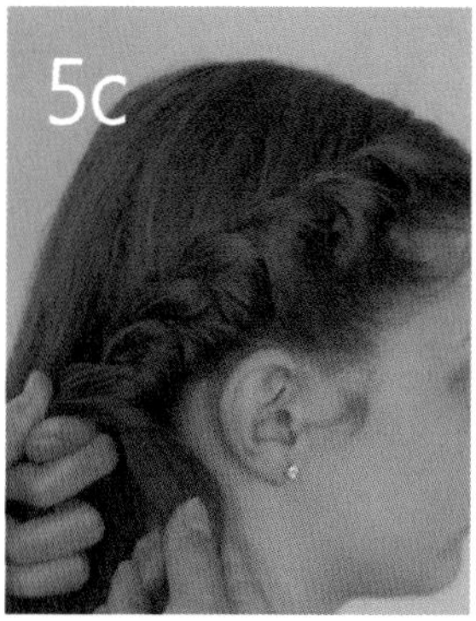

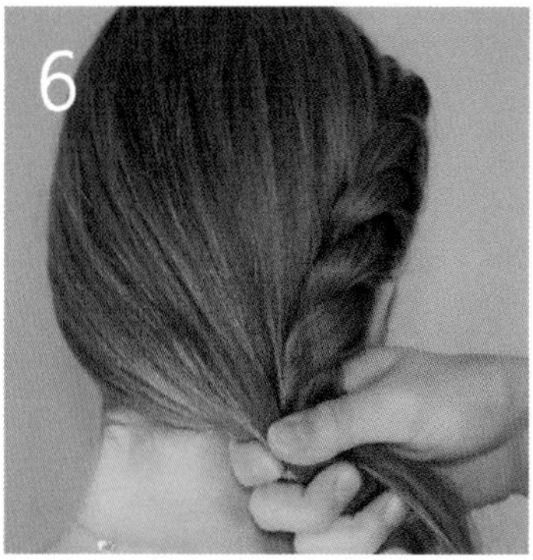

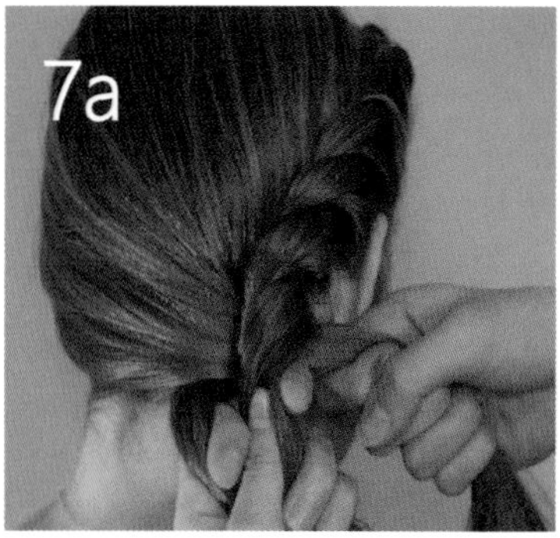

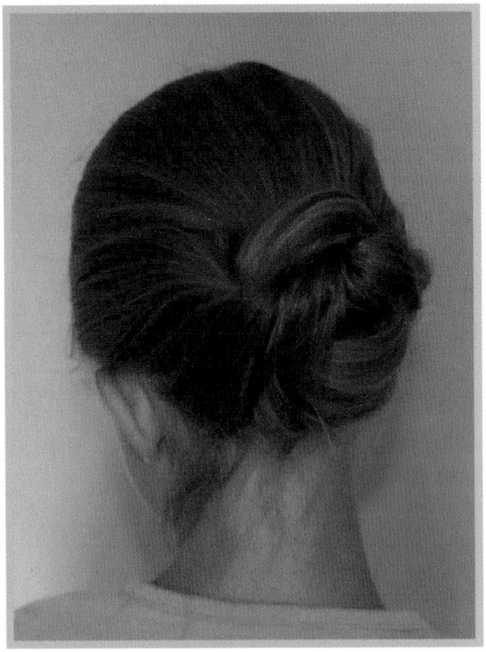

Topsy Tail Bun

This elegant bun is so simple to create. To make this bun you will need a Topsy Tail styling tool.

1. Pull all of the hair back into a low ponytail. Secure the pony with a large clear elastic hair-tie. Keep it fairly loose.

2. Take the Topsy Tail and insert the pointed part into the hair right above the elastic hair-tie (see picture).

3. Thread the entire ponytail through the loop of the Topsy Tail.

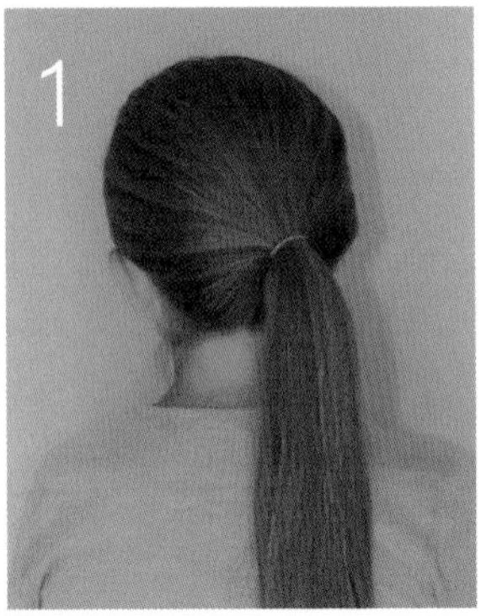

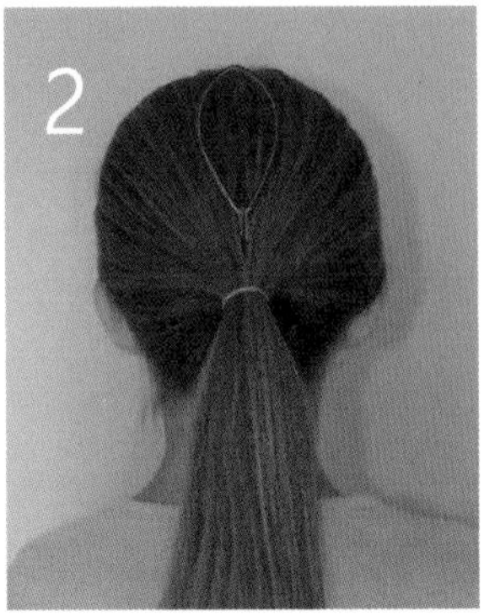

4. Now firmly pull the Topsy Tail down through the hair, flipping the ponytail. You will now have two little twists on either side of the ponytail.

5. Divide the ponytail into two equal sections.

6. Cross the right-hand section over the left-hand section, trading places

7. Take the Topsy Tail and insert the pointed part up through the twist on the left side (see picture).

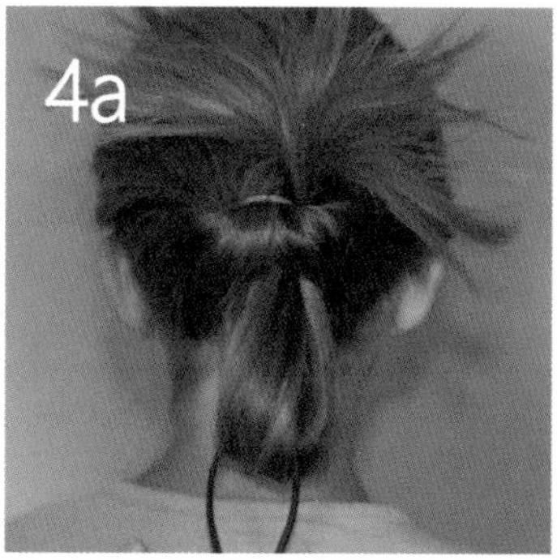

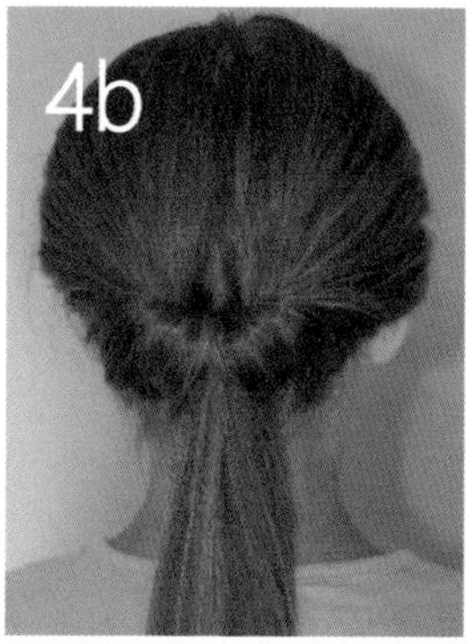

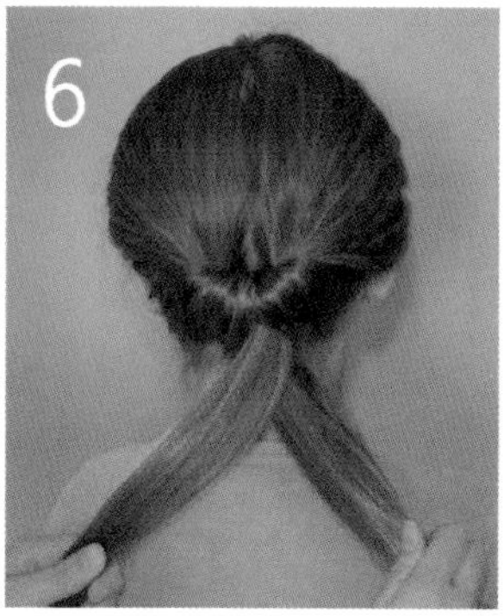

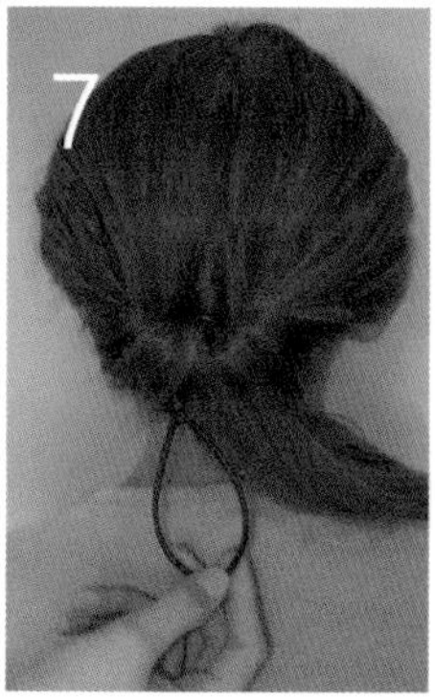

8. Thread the left-hand section through the loop of the Topsy Tail. Pull the Topsy Tail up through the twist.

9. Keeping the hair still threaded through the loop, insert the Topsy Tail, pointed part down, through the twist on the right side. Pull the Topsy Tail down through the twist.

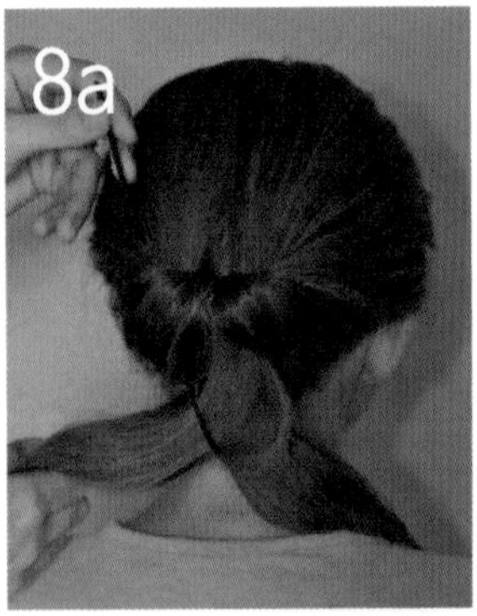

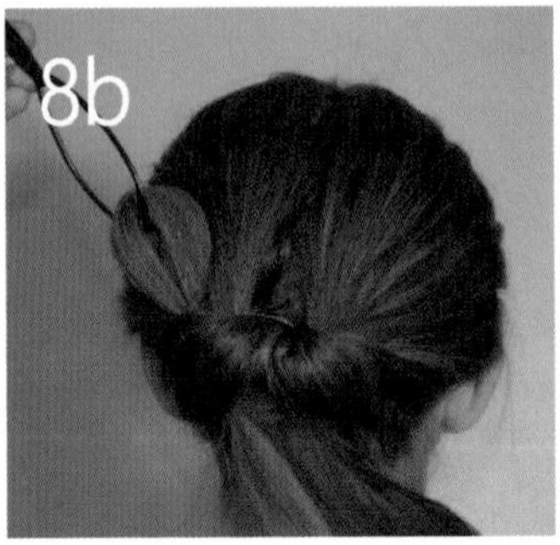

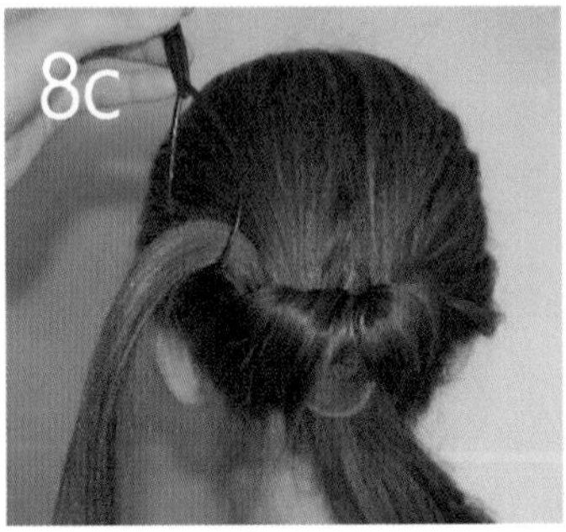

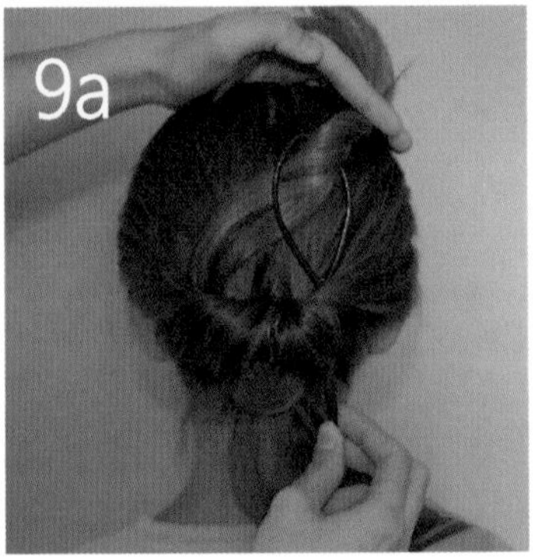

10. Keeping the hair still threaded through the loop, insert the Topsy Tail, pointed part up, through the twist on the left side once again. Pull the Topsy Tail up through the twist.

11. Depending on how long your hair is, you may need to repeat steps 9-10. Stop when you have 2 inches of hair left. Tuck the ends underneath the bun and secure with bobby pins.

12. Repeat steps 7-10 with the remaining section of hair except go the opposite way, starting at the twist on the right side. Again, depending on how long your hair is, repeat steps 9-10 until you have only 2 inches of hair left.

13. Tuck the ends underneath the bun and secure with bobby pins. Use bobby pins to pin stray hairs and secure the bun.

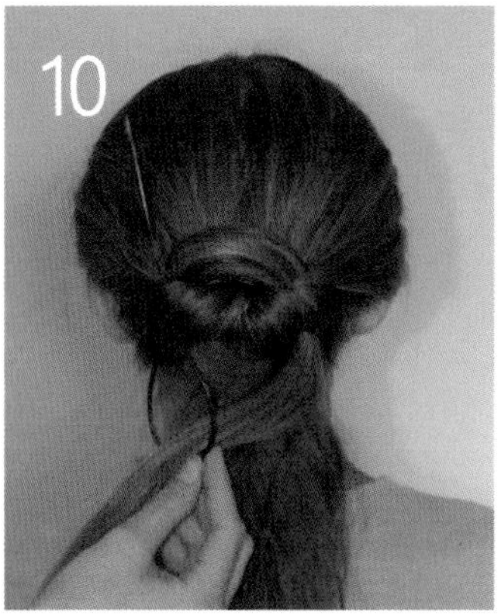

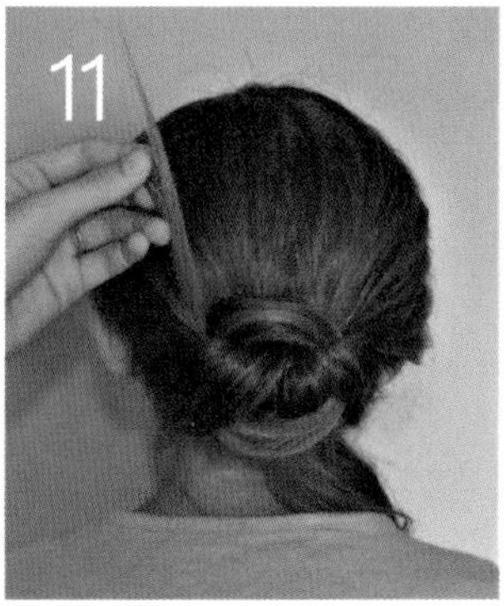

Messy Bun

There are many different ways to make a messy bun, but this version works great for those with long hair.

1. We will start this style by creating a Bubble Braid. Gather hair into a low ponytail and secure with a clear elastic.

2. About 2 inches down from the base of the pony, tie a clear elastic around the ponytail.

3. Spilt the section of hair in between the elastics, into two sections.

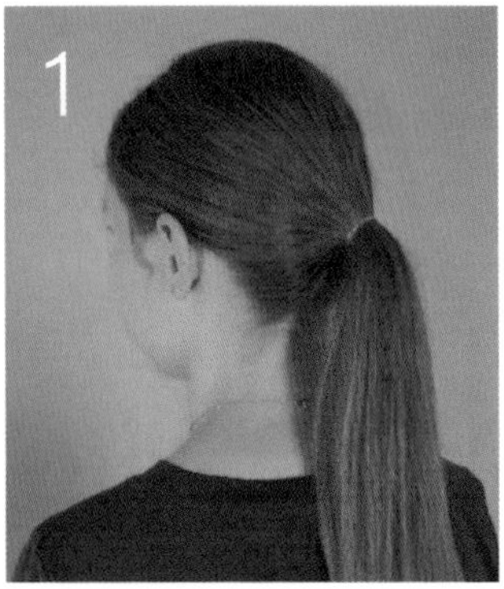

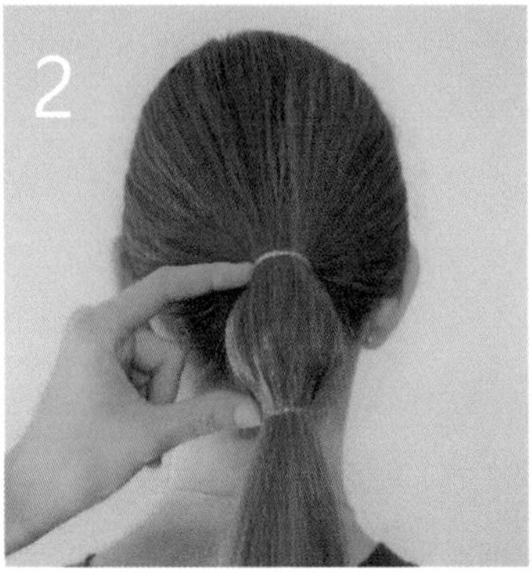

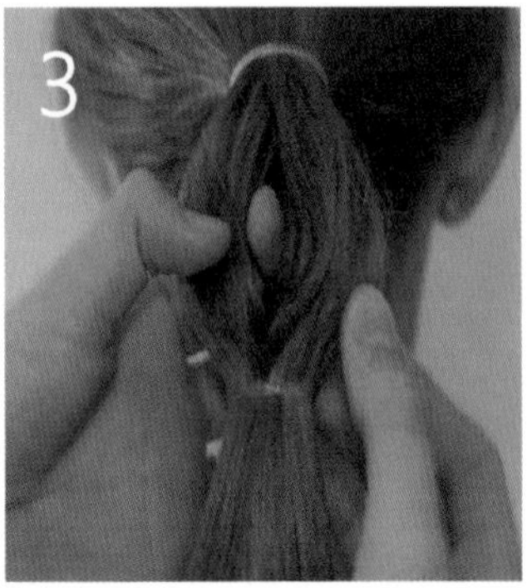

4. Pull the ponytail up and through the hole you have created, flipping it.

5. Go about 2 inches down and tie another clear elastic around the ponytail. Complete steps 3-4 again, making another "bubble."

6. Continue making "bubbles" down the ponytail. Stop when you have 2 inches of ends left. Tie off braid with a clear elastic. Pancake the edges of the braid.

7. Now to make the messy bun. Take the braid and wrap it up around the elastic at the base of the pony. Tuck the ends underneath the bun and secure with bobby pins. Pin the bun in place by using bobby pins.

8. Position, pull, and pin the hair until it meets your liking. Remember that this is a messy bun. It does not need to look perfect.

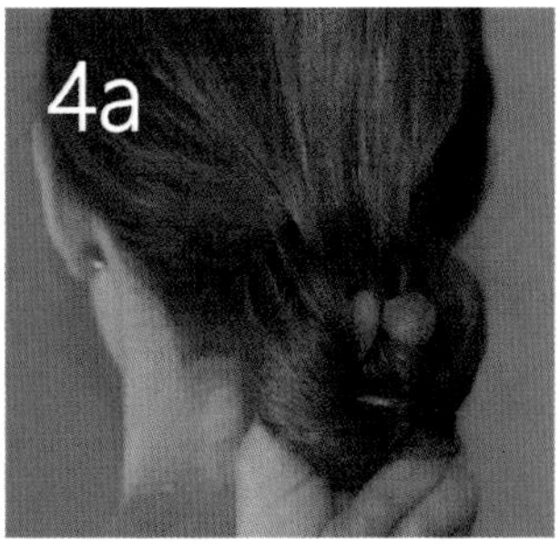

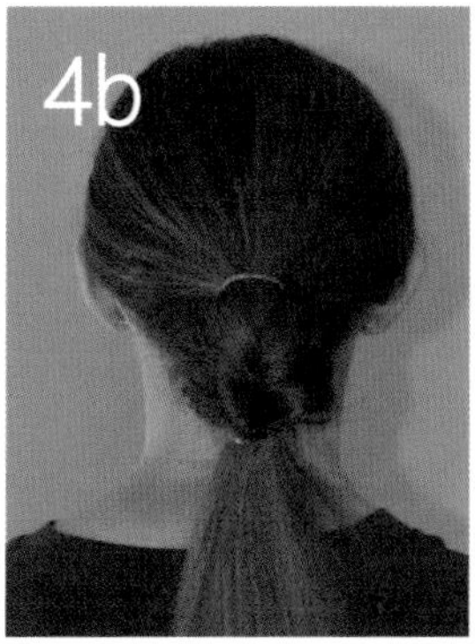

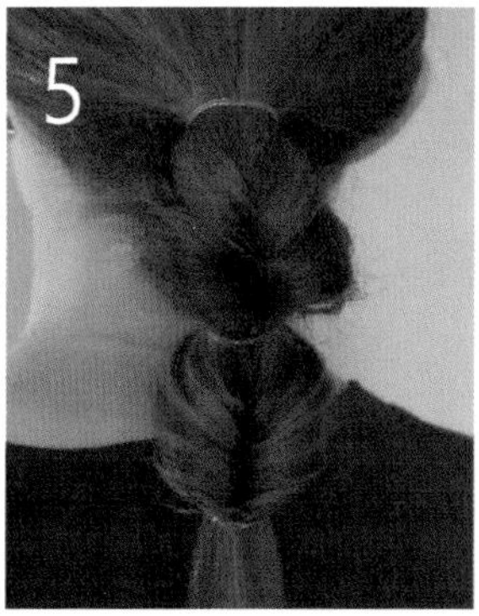

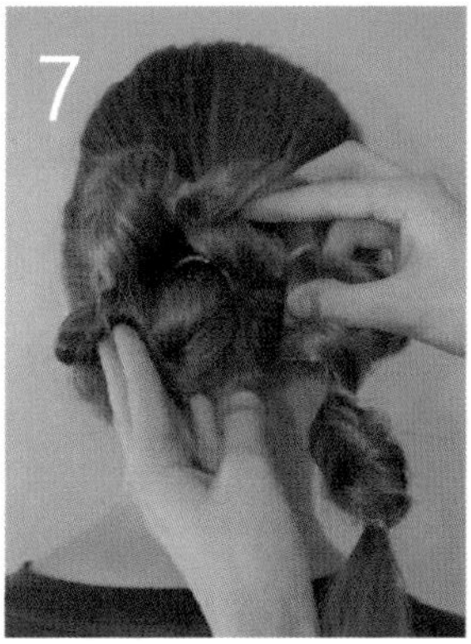

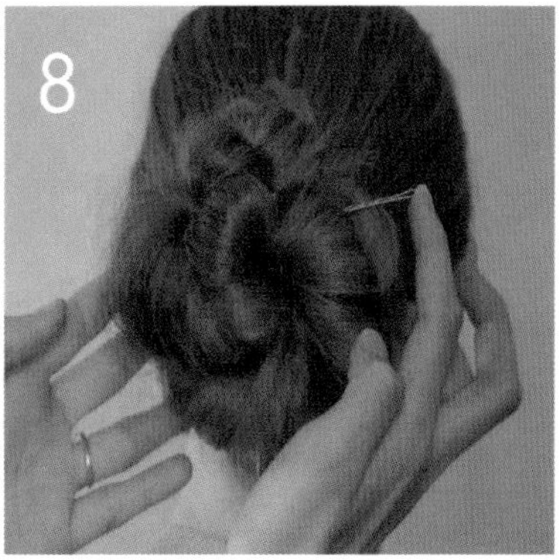

Fishtail Braid

Also known as a Fishbone Braid, this braid has an intricate, unique look that sets it apart from other braids. It Is important to take small sections of hair as it really gives it the "fishtail" look.

1. Divide hair into two equal sections.

2. Take a small section of hair from the outside edge of the left-hand section. Cross this section OVER to the right-hand section of hair.

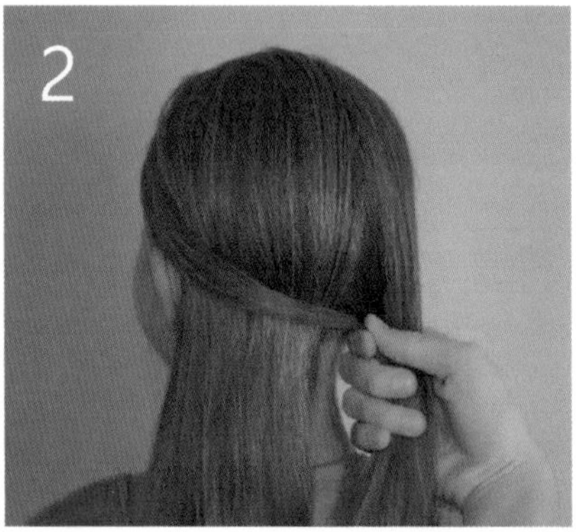

3. Now take a small section of hair from the outside edge of the right-hand section. Cross this section OVER to the left-hand section. You have completed one "rotation" of a Fishtail Braid.

4. Continue steps 2-3 until you run out of hair. Each time you go to take a strand it will be from what is in the opposite hand. Make sure that when you cross the small sections over you keep it tight. You can go back after the braid is finished and pancake the edges a little bit to loosen the braid.

5. Secure ends with a clear elastic.

Hair Variations

Fishtail braids also make amazing buns! Pancake the edges of the braid and wrap it up into a bun for messy look. To create a sleek and formal bun, spritz hair with water before braiding to reduce flyaways.

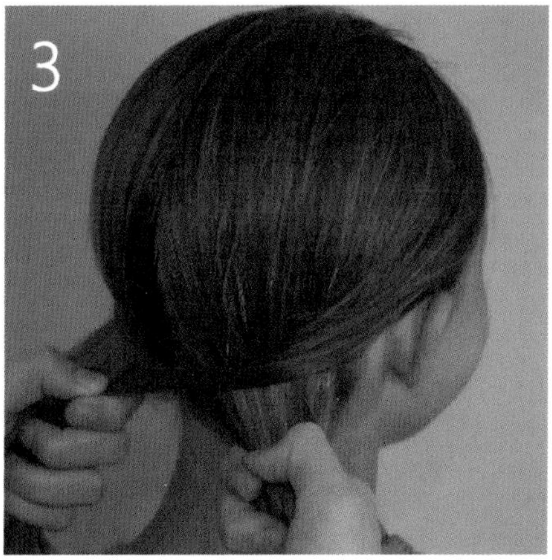

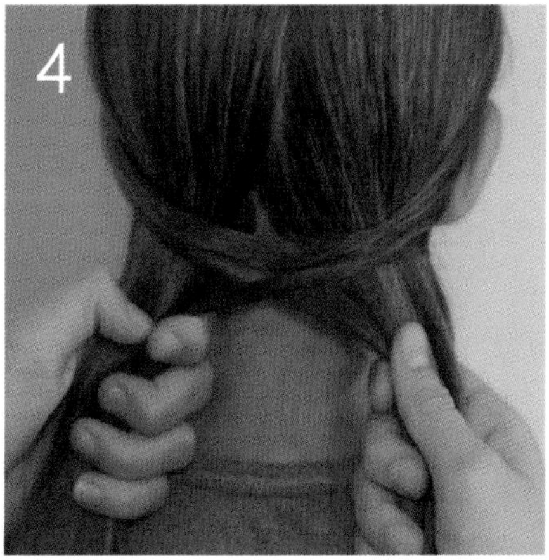

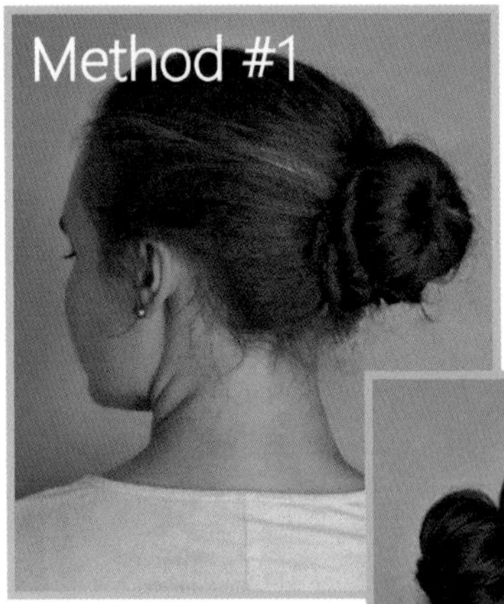

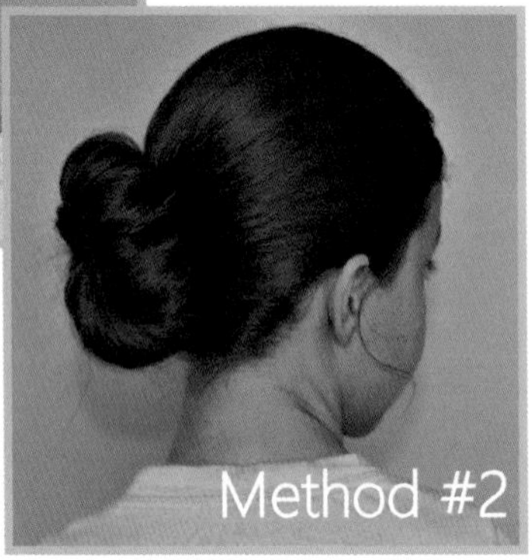

Donut Bun

There are two ways to create a donut bun. Method #1 can work for short to medium length hair, and Method #2 works best for those with long hair.

Method #1

1. Use a hair-tie to secure all of the hair in a mid-pony at the back of the head.

2. Pull the entire ponytail through the hole in the middle of the bun former so that covers the hair-tie.

3. Tilt the head down, chin toward chest, and spread the hair evenly over the shape of the bun former (see picture).

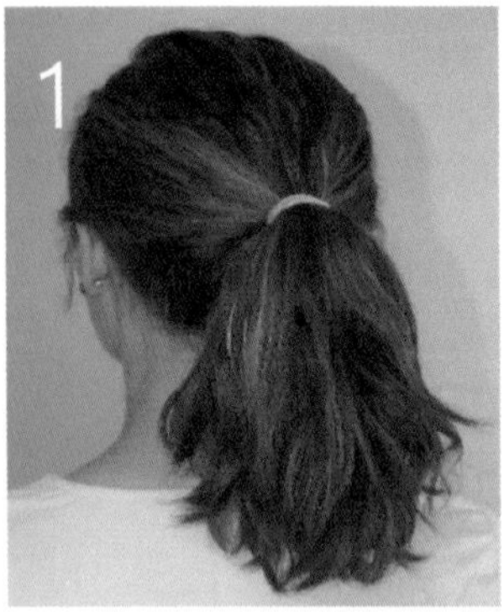

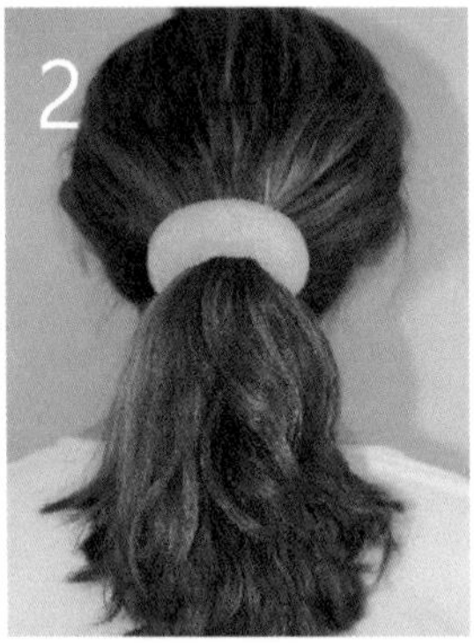

4. Take a large clear elastic and stretch it over and around the bun, securing the hair covering the bun former. Make sure that the bun former is completely covered with the hair.

5. Gather the ends of the hair down beneath the bun (see picture 5a). Divide the hair into two sections (see picture 5b).

6. Twist the right-hand section of hair and wrap it clockwise around the bun. Try to cover the elastic. Bobby pin the end of the twist in place. Repeat with the left-hand section but wrap this section counter-clockwise around the bun. Make sure that the entire bun is secure by pinning it in place with bobby pins.

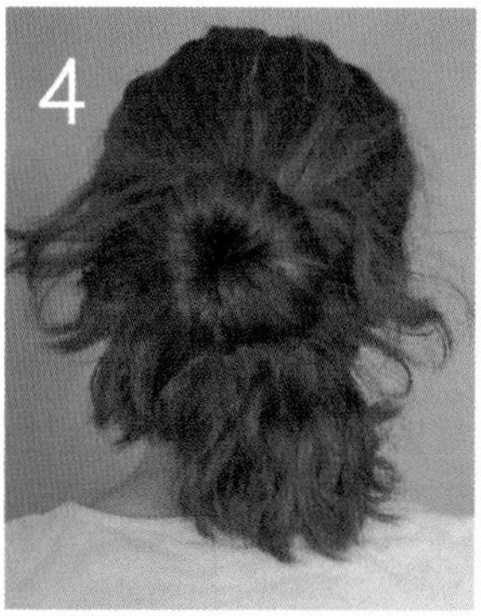

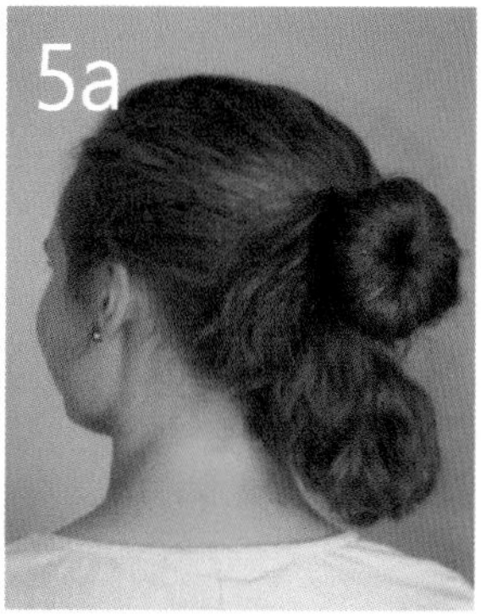

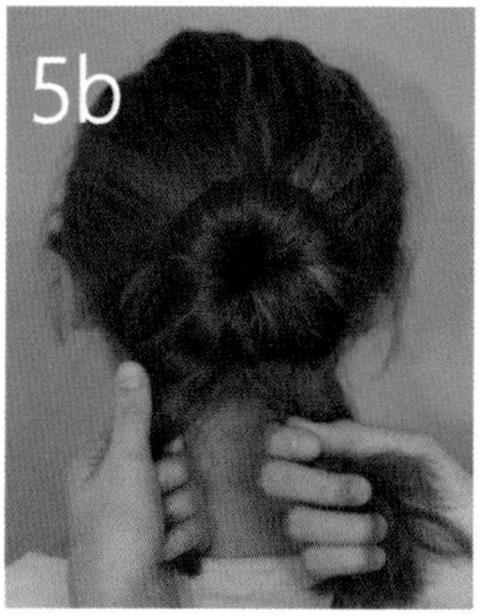

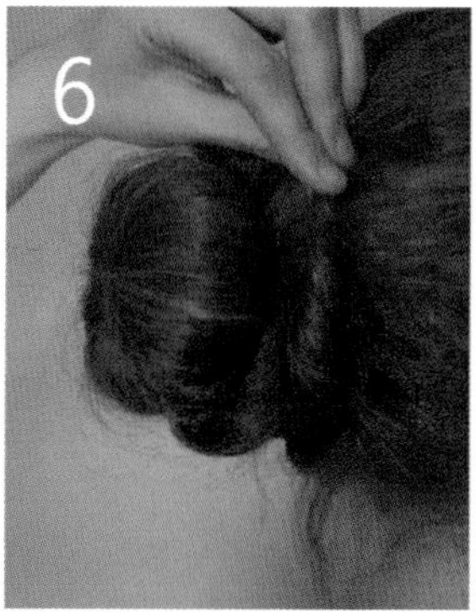

Method #2

1. Use a hair-tie to secure all of the hair into mid-pony at the back of the head. Make sure the hair in the ponytail is smooth.

2. Pull the entire ponytail through the middle of the bun former. Then bring the bun former down the ponytail so that you have 4-5 inches of hair left hanging out.

3. Spread the ends of the hair over the bun former and tuck the ends under (see picture).

4. Taking the bun former, roll it up the ponytail, so that the hair is tucked and rolled around the bun former (see picture). Make sure that you keep the hair being wrapped around tight and not loose. You can do this by pulling down on the ponytail while rolling the bun former.

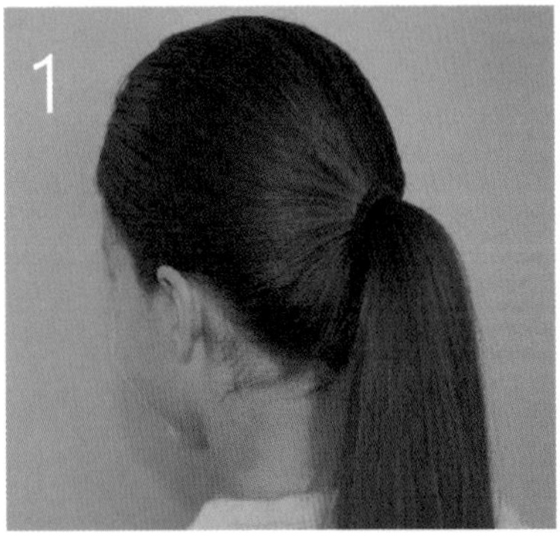

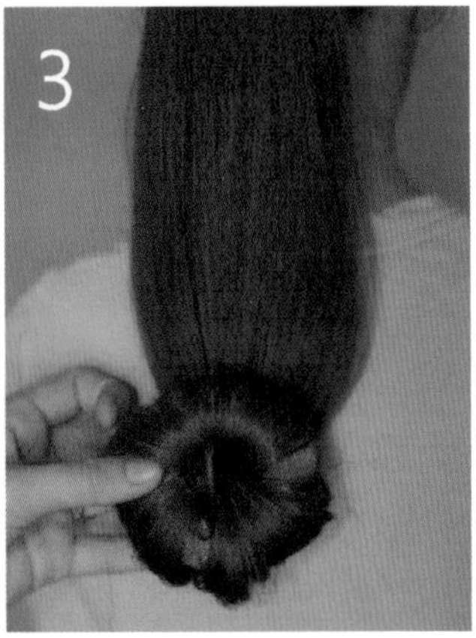

5. Once you have wrapped all the hair from the ponytail around the bun former, roll a few more times close to head to make sure that the bun will stay in place on the back of the head.

6. If needed, bobby pin the bun to the back of the head so that it feels secure.

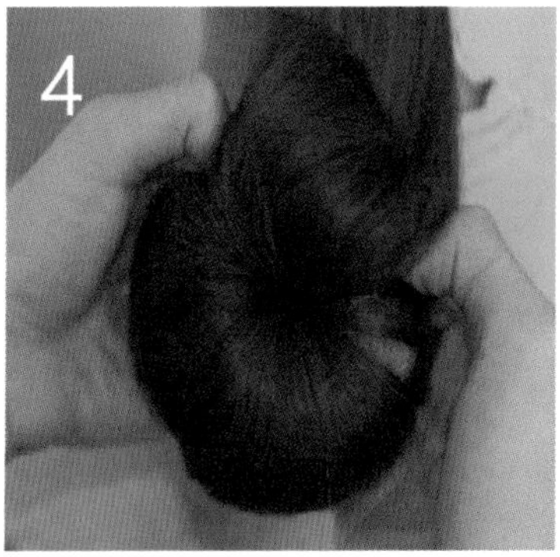

Hair Variations

Depending on if you want a higher bun or a lower bun, just place the ponytail in the desired position and create your bun.

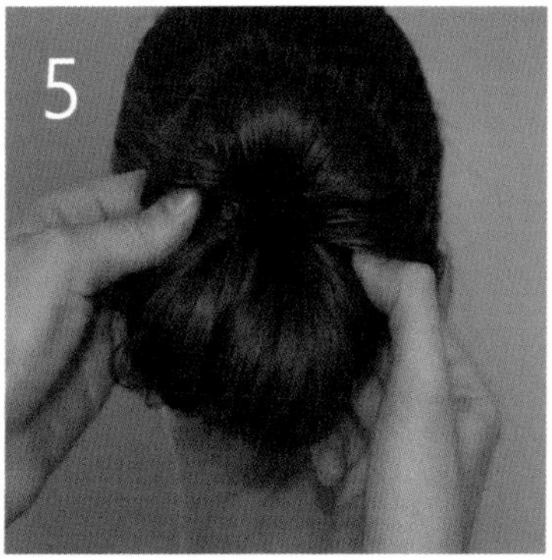

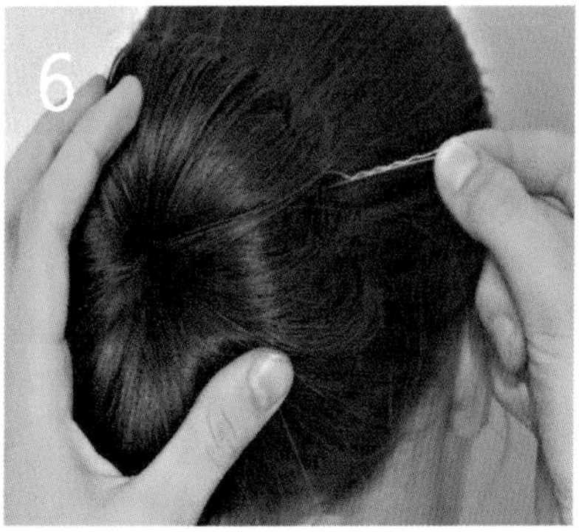

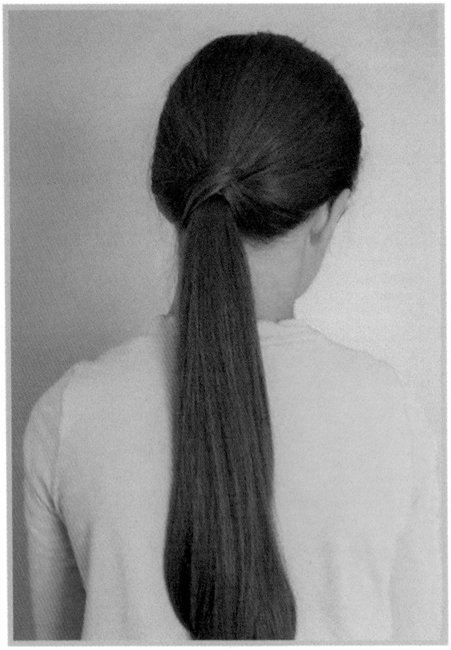

Criss-Cross Pony

This sophisticated style is the perfect way to glam up your ponytail. This style uses a Topsy Tail to create the crisscross look.

1. Lift up hair and create a section underneath that goes from ear to ear (see picture 1a). Divide this section into two equal strands and place each over a shoulder, out of the way.

2. Gather the rest of the hair into a low ponytail, close to the nape of the neck. Secure with a large elastic hair-tie.

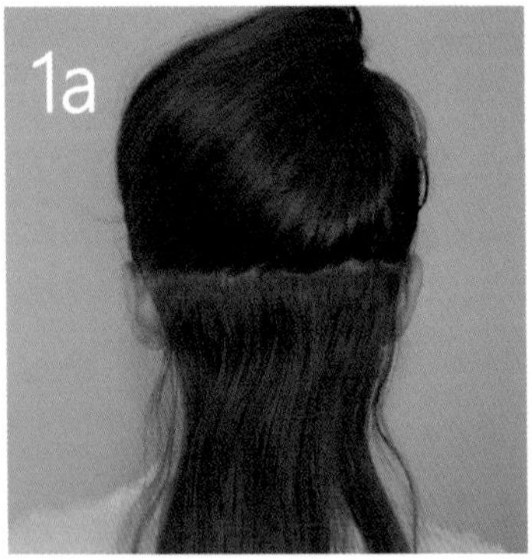

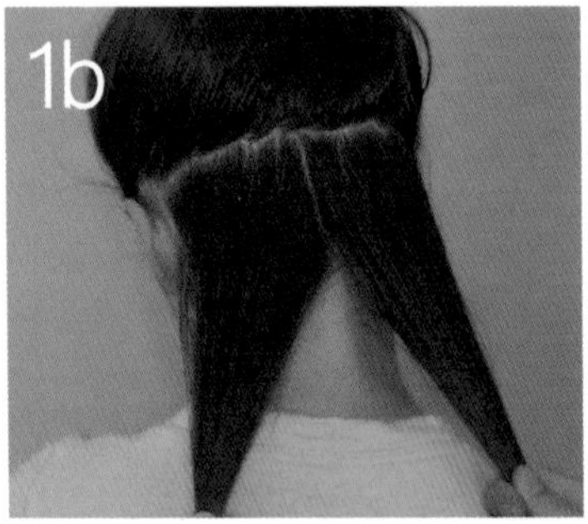

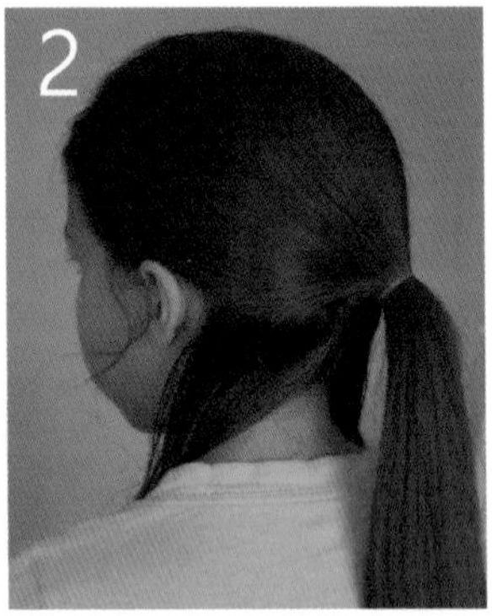

3. Taking your Topsy Tail, insert the pointed part into the hair left of the elastic hair-tie, at a slight angle (see picture).

4. Now take the right-hand strand and thread it up and through the loop. Pull the Topsy Tail down through the hair.

5. Repeat steps 3-4, inserting the Topsy Tail in the hair right of the hair-tie, and pulling the left-hand strand of hair through.

6. Make sure the two strands are underneath the ponytail so that they get secured in step seven.

7. Take a clear elastic hair-tie and secure the entire ponytail with the two strands underneath. Tighten the ponytail so that the crisscross covers the elastic hair-tie.

Hair Variations

To make this style a bit more formal, curl the ponytail and leave some hairs loose about the face.

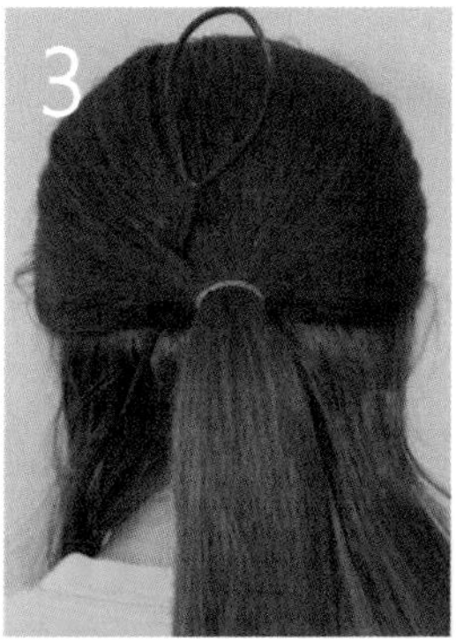

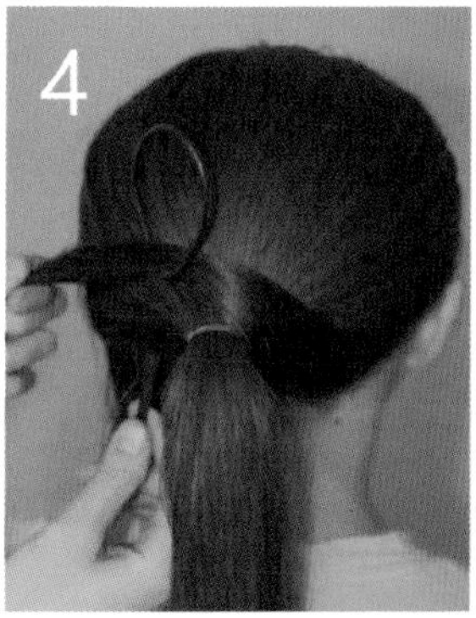

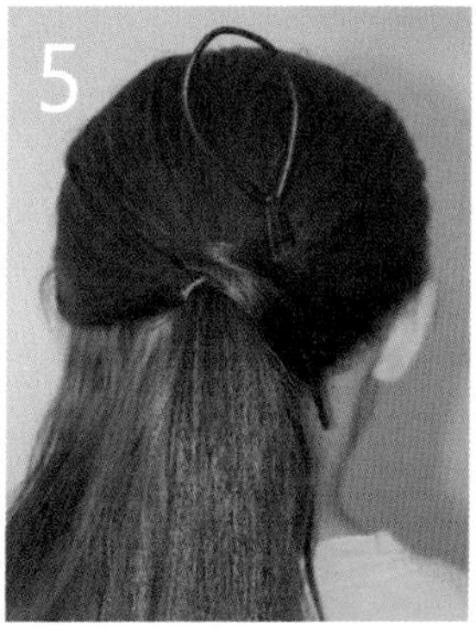

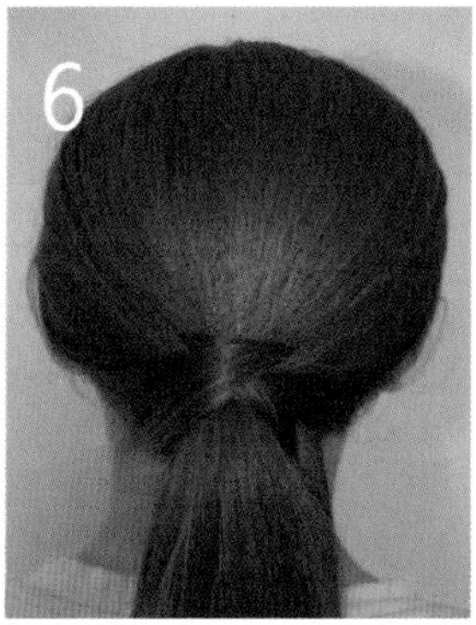

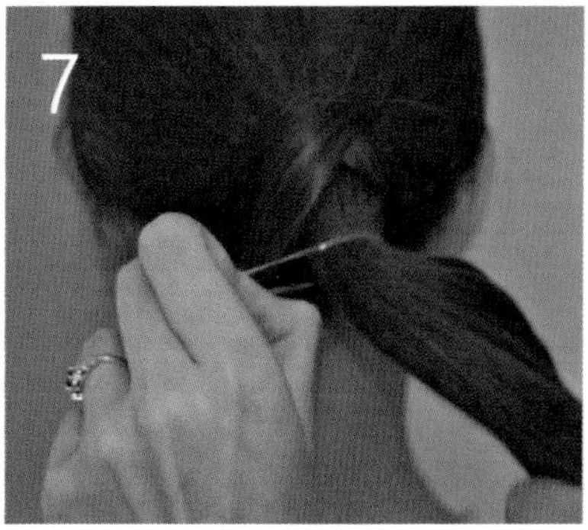

Abbi Robertson is a homeschool student living with her family in West Phoenix on a small hobby "farm." As the oldest child of seven, Abbi's time is filled with school, chores, looking after little brothers, and lots of laughter. She started to have an interest in hairstyling at age 13 and has been building her skills since then. This book is a compilation of the styles that she began creating when she first started to do her own hair. Abbi's purpose for this book and everything she does, is to bring glory to her Creator and to encourage and bring joy to those around her.

20930626R00028

Printed in Great Britain
by Amazon